THE SAMUEL AND ALTHEA STROUM LECTURES
IN JEWISH STUDIES

THE SAMUEL AND ALTHEA STROUM LECTURES
IN JEWISH STUDIES

The Yiddish Art Song, performed by Leon Lishner, basso,
and Lazar Weiner, piano (stereophonic record album)

The Holocaust in Historical Perspective, by Yehuda Bauer

The Holocaust
in Historical Perspective

YEHUDA BAUER

UNIVERSITY OF WASHINGTON PRESS

Seattle

Library of Congress Cataloging in Publication Data
Bauer, Yehuda.
    The holocaust in historical perspective.

    (Samuel and Althea Stroum lectures in Jewish studies)
    Includes index.
    1. Holocaust, Jewish (1939–1945)—Addresses, essays, lectures. 2. Holocaust, Jewish (1939–1945)—Historiography—Addresses, essays, lectures. 3. Jews in the United States—Politics and government—Addresses, essays, lectures. 4. Brand, Joel, 1906–1964—Addresses, essays, lectures. 5. United States—Politics and government—1933–1945—Addresses, essays, lectures.
I. Title. II. Series.
D810.J4B315824   940.S3'1503'924   78-2988
ISBN 0-295-95606-2

THE SAMUEL AND ALTHEA STROUM LECTURES

IN JEWISH STUDIES

Samuel Stroum, businessman, community leader, and philanthropist, by a major gift to the Jewish Federation of Greater Seattle, established the Samuel and Althea Stroum Philanthropic Fund.

In recognition of Mr. and Mrs. Stroum's deep interest in Jewish history and culture, the Board of Directors of the Jewish Federation of Seattle, in cooperation with the Jewish Studies Program of the University of Washington, established an annual lectureship at the University of Washington known as the Samuel and Althea Stroum Lectureship in Jewish Studies. This lectureship makes it possible to bring to the area outstanding scholars and interpreters of Jewish thought, thus promoting a deeper understanding of Jewish history, religion, and culture. Such understanding can lead to an enhanced appreciation of the Jewish contributions to the historical and cultural traditions that have shaped the American nation.

The terms of the gift also provide for the publication from time to time of the lectures or other appropriate materials resulting from or related to the lectures.

Acknowledgments

I should like to express my deep appreciation to Mr. Samuel N. and Mrs. Althea Stroum of Seattle, who made it possible for me to come to Seattle and deliver the essays contained in this book in the form of lectures in the lecture series bearing their name; and to Professors Edward Alexander and Deborah E. Lipstadt of the Jewish Studies Program at the University of Washington, who provided the academic framework and helped to determine the topics of these lectures.

Contents

THE HOLOCAUST IN HISTORICAL PERSPECTIVE

Introduction

WHY IS THE HOLOCAUST A CENTRAL EXPERIENCE OF
our civilization? Is it because what could happen once, can
happen again? Is it because modern technology has helped
to uncover hidden and frightening recesses of man's potential for evil? Is it because we have seen how people can
become enmeshed in a bureaucratic hell which leads them
into the negation first of themselves and then of others? Is
it because we see in the Holocaust the heights of the
human spirit as well as its abysses? Is it because some of us
ask where was God, and others ask where was Man?

It is these and similar questions that cause more and
more people to devote their attention to the Holocaust,
the mass murder of the Jewish people during the Nazi
period. The great philosophical questions can be posed,
but very few of them can be satisfactorily answered. There
is a distinct danger of escaping from the reality of the Nazi
regime and its consequences into a nebulous general humanism, where all persecutions become holocausts, and
where a general and meaningless condemnation of evil
helps to establish a curtain between oneself and the real
thing. This escapism must of course be fought.

The essays in this volume try to present different aspects
of this general theme: the return to the actual reality and
concreteness of the Holocaust. This reality can be grasped

through a historical viewpoint, though there certainly are other ways to do so as well; an artistic, or literary approach, an approach through the film medium—all these suggest themselves as valid alternatives. What is claimed therefore is not the exclusiveness of the historical perspective, but its legitimacy as one of the possible ways in which to try to grapple with what cannot be fully grasped. Quite possibly, the historical perspective may have the additional advantage of easing the way to awareness for generations that have come after the searing fate of the actual experience. Were the Holocaust to remain the province of only those who were direct witnesses, it would not become the terrible warning for all the rest of us that it should be.

The historical perspective demands, first of all, a basic knowledge of stark facts. It is so easy to indulge in generalities—but one has to know the where and when and how and in what sequence. When one lives in a Western society, one wonders how the information of what was happening Over There was obtained here, and how it was received. Therefore, the first of the essays in this volume deals with the Holocaust itself—a summary, and a warning: what is information, and when and how does information become knowledge?

It is necessary to dispel mystification around the Holocaust, if only to clear the way for the historical perspective. There are a number of such possible mystifications, including one that involves the historic approach itself. A proper understanding of the pitfalls involved in following the natural tendency of human beings to obfuscate that which is highly unpleasant to face head on is essential if the historical examination is to have any real value. There is a need to warn against false overemotionalism and mythological extravagances. There is equally a need to warn against self-serving falsifications which of late seem to appear from all corners of the earth. The old calumny of the Jews somehow having murdered themselves is not the least of these. But one has, in all honesty, to warn also against the growing tendency of immersing tears and suffering in oceans of footnotes, of coming up with a remote quasi-scientific approach which could be as inhuman as that of those who committed the crime or of those who stood by and watched indifferently.

Once the mystifications have been explained, it is time to move into samples of what a historical perspective might mean. Two topics have been examined in order to show two possible ways of approach. One is the approach of generalization, of trying to see whether patterns exist in that vast sea of events that was the Holocaust. The topic chosen to illustrate this line of approach is a basic one: the interrelationship of Jew and Gentile, inside the Holocaust realm and outside it. Obviously, with such a vast overall subject, all that can be attempted is a sketch and the delineation of a basic framework. What is important is a methodology—trying to see whether patterns exist—and a first intimation of the vast problems raised by formulating the relevant questions.

The last piece is intended to be indicative of the other methodology that suggests itself in an analysis of the Holocaust: the examination of a central but limited topic in great detail and based on as varied source material as is possible. This examination, for which a hitherto unexplored and tragically fascinating event in Holocaust history was chosen, leads to the posing of some disturbing, even frightening, questions. The story of the Brand mission is really the story of Cain and Abel. The blood of the brother was crying out from the earth. Was the civilized Christian world the keeper of its elder Jewish brother? If not, why not? The problem as posed in the essay itself is seemingly pragmatic, not general, certainly not philosophical. But the general and philosophical have been kept in mind when dealing with the involved details of what either is a moral problem, or could be written as a spy story. One hopes that the latter eventuality will not come about.

Thus, the thread running through our story is that of an attempt at understanding of the Holocaust through the historical perspective: fact, de-mystification, and interpretation. The Holocaust was vast, and so must its historiography be. It cannot be encompassed in one book, or one history. The only alternative is to light it up from one of the possible angles, in a paradigmatic way rather than as a fully unfolding story. This is what is being essayed in this volume.

1. The Holocaust and American Jewry

THE UNIQUE QUALITY OF NAZI JEW-HATRED WAS SOME-thing so surprising, so outside of the experience of the civilized world, that the Jewish leadership as well as the Jewish people could not comprehend it. Unbelievingly, and therefore outwitted at every turn of the Nazi screw, they stood by and watched with ever-increasing despair as Nazi policy moved from one phase to the next. The post-Holocaust generation has difficulty understanding this basic psychological barrier to action on the part of Jews—and non-Jews—during the Nazi period. We already know what happened, and that mass murder was possible; they, who lived at that time, did not. For them it was a totally new reality that was unfolding before their shocked eyes and paralyzed minds. It was literally unbelievable, because it was unexpected and unprecedented. And yet, of course, it had roots and a background. Nobody predicted it; all quotations purporting to show that this or that statesman or thinker predicted the Holocaust are taken out of context. Words such as "extinction" or "destruction" were meant to convey images of pogroms, economic destruction, hunger, or forced emigration. They were meant to indicate the untenability of the Jewish position in Europe. They did not indicate a knowledge or a serious prediction of the mass murder of millions of human beings.

7

Nazi attitudes to Jews were colored by the extreme forms of antisemitism* that developed towards the end of the nineteenth century. Nurtured by a society in crisis, a cultural pessimism developed that sought to eradicate the moral restraints of accepted religion. At the margins of such ideological developments there arose people who, using and transforming Christian stereotypes of Jews as symbols of the Devil that had been transmitted for many centuries, satisfied the need of the disoriented elements in the industrial society for a clearly defined Devil-figure to concentrate their hatred on: they found, or refound, the Jew. The Jew they pictured as the incarnation of evil, the bearer of social and even physical disease, the germ that brought sickness and destruction upon cultures, the ugly Lucifer trying to rape and thereby sully and contaminate non-Jewish women. The Jew was a germ; not really a human being at all. "You are no human, you are no dog, you are a Jew," said a Gestapo official to a member of the Warsaw Jewish Council in late 1939.[1] The Jew was vermin, the Jew was anti-race; he was both a demoniac concept and also a real, visible enemy. Richard Wagner, the musician and forerunner of Hitler, declared that it was only through weakness in German society that the Jews could take root in it and its strengthening would inevitably mean their removal. "The Jew is always within us," said Hitler, "but it is easier to combat him in the flesh than as the invisible demon."[2]

Jew-hatred was the central pillar of a pseudoreligion that transformed accepted moral values into their opposite,

---

* We prefer the spelling "antisemitism" to "anti-Semitism," in order to avoid the implication that there is a "Semitism" to which Jew-haters are opposed. In fact, the term "antisemitism" was coined in the late seventies of the nineteenth century by individuals who were looking for a pseudoscientific term for "Jew hatred," which had come to sound barbaric. Antisemites do not hate Semites; they hate Jews.

but within a framework of accepted and traditional ideas. The pseudoreligion was clearly inspired by Christian symbols, but subverted and changed them completely. Using these Christian symbols in a sacrilegious way, modern antisemitism, and especially Nazism of course, could use terms, quotations, and associations that were familiar to the Christian-educated mind. The unity of God the Father, God the Son, and the Holy Ghost became the Nazi "Father of the State, the Son of the Race and the Spirit of the Volk." [3] The image of the Jew as the symbol of the Devil in some of the premodern traditions made it easy to transform the Jew into the Devil himself, the content of the symbol, and thus to lead to the obvious conclusion that he had to be destroyed. When the Fuhrer became the substitute for the Saviour, the former symbol of the anti-Christ became the target of an absolute hatred. The modern imagery fitted old concepts. The Jews were depicted as always being enemies of order and revolutionaries, while at the same time being capitalists. The Jews were not really nomads, but parasites, "battening on the substance of others." [4]

Of course, one does not argue with parasites. But the logic that led to a policy of murder was not necessarily perceived. The forerunners of Hitler's antisemitism had advocated the forcible extirpation of the Jews as early as the beginning of the last century. [5] The demand was repeated several times in the course of the latter part of the century, and early in the twentieth. Eugen Duhring and others vied with each other in extreme formulations. Hitler himself demanded the removal of the Jews (*Entfernung*) as early as 1919. But contrary to the claims of some historians, it is by no means clear whether he meant murder or forced emigration from German soil. In his book *Mein Kampf,* as in his talks with Rauschning and in his speeches, with all their extreme antisemitism, there is no clear indication of an actual murderous design. "I asked whether this meant that the Jew should be exterminated completely," said Rauschning. "No," replied Hitler, "if that were the case we should have to invent him. One needs a visible enemy, not just an invisible one."[6] It seems that not even in Hitler's own mind was there a clear picture of what exactly should be done with the Jews until fairly late; it would have required an uncanny prescience on the part of Jews or others to deduct from what appeared to be the unclear and imprecise, if ominous and threatening, ravings of an extreme antisemite, the precise outlines of mass murder. Jews reacted to present threat with reference to past experience; what they were threatened with were persecutions, pogroms perhaps, hunger, economic destruction. It was this threat they were trying to combat.

Two weapons employed by Nazism were so-called racism and a system of cover-up by symbolic use of language. Nazi racism was actually based on just two thoughts. One was that there was good blood or bad; the term "blood" being used in the mystical sense as a transmitter of inherent moral and cultural as well as physical qualities. Good blood was Germanic blood. Transcending German nationalism, though basing itself on it, Nazi ideology derived all positive qualities from a supposed Aryan background, but this only served as cover-up for the claim of Germanic (German, Nordic, Scandinavian, etc.) blood to rule the world by conquering the land mass of Eastern Europe and utilizing its tremendous natural resources. "Aryan" actually had only the quality of distinguishing it from "non-Aryan"; the only non-Aryan was the Jew. Antisemitism was therefore not a result of Nazi racism, but the obverse was true: racism was a rationalization of Jew-hatred.

Language itself was corrupted and changed to fit Nazi aims. The term "antisemitism" had been invented by Wilhelm Marr in 1879 in order to call Jew-hatred by a modern, acceptable name which would not mention Jews at all. Similar uses of language covered up for aims and purposes of Nazism as they slowly developed. Deception became an art, perhaps the only art at which Nazis excelled. Yet on the other hand there was also unwitting deception, in that the Nazis themselves had no clear notion of the ultimate aims of their Jewish policies.

Nazi policy towards the Jews developed in stages, but that does not mean that there was a clearly preconceived plan, nor that at any given turning point there were not other options open to the Nazis that were considered seriously; there developed in Nazi Germany only one clear idea regarding Jews that was accepted by all policy makers, namely the idea that ultimately the Jews had no place in Germany. This however was not just a Nazi idea—even in the plans for a future Germany discussed during the war by the right-wing opposition to Hitler there was no room for any Jews. The removal of Jews from German soil was the one idea that persisted to the very end: when Himmler met with Norbert Masur of the World Jewish Congress at the end of the war, desperately trying to create an alibi for himself, he still stuck to the notion that there was no room for Jews in Germany.[7]

It is possible to differentiate between a number of phases of Nazi policy in the thirties up to the outbreak of war: a first stage, characterized by the boycott of April 1933, in which a direct assault on the Jews was attempted and abandoned; a second, characterized by slowly mounting pressure interspersed with periods of seeming stabilization, which lasted until the November pogrom of 1938; and a stage of active persecution and forced emigration between the pogrom and the outbreak of war. All three phases were marked by the desire of the Nazis to push the Jews out of the economy and the society, expropriate them and force them out. Until the November pogrom (*Reichskristallnacht*) Jews had not generally been arrested as Jews, and put into the concentration camps. Most Jews in the camps prior to that date were there because of their political anti-Nazi activities. This changed with the pogrom, and the camps were used as an effective method of terrorizing the Jews into speedier emigration. At the same time the first rumblings of violent solutions were heard. The nonhuman quality of the Jews was emphasized ("the Jew is not a human being; he is a sign of rottenness," declared Walter Buch, the Nazi party-judge in 1938);[8] and the ss periodical *Das Schwarze Korps* said in an article of 24 November 1938 that now that the Jews were about to be removed from the German economy they might well descend into poverty and criminality, in which case "we would be faced with the hard necessity to exterminate the Jewish underworld in the way we generally exterminate crime in our well-ordered state: with fire and sword. The result would be the actual and final end of Jewry in Germany, its complete destruction." Yet this was an isolated expression in writing, just as Hitler's famous speech of 30 January 1939, in which he threatened the "Jewish race" in Europe with destruction if it "instigated" another world war, was an isolated instance of an oral threat. The German foreign ministry advised its missions abroad in an official circular of 25 January 1939 that emigration of Jews would be advanced with every possible means because this would export antisemitism and thus create sympathy abroad for Germany. The Schacht-Rublee plan of the same winter, which was designed to solve the question of German Jewry by emigration in return for the advancement of German exports coupled with a virtual expropriation of German Jewry, was also approved by Hitler.[9]

The period of 1939 to 1941 was another phase in Nazi policy towards Jews. Emigration was fostered and pushed despite the outbreak of war, but it depended of course upon the willingness of the West to accept the Jews. The West was obviously not willing, and the Nazis began to adopt the "territorial final solution." First came an attempt to settle the Jews on the new German-Soviet border where many of them would be pushed into neighboring Russia—the Lublin-Nisko scheme. This was tried between September 1939, when it clearly lay behind Heydrich's instructions of 21 September 1939 to establish ghettos and Jewish Councils near railway centers in preparation for a final aim yet to be spelled out, and April 1940, when the opposition of the Nazi ruler of Poland, Hans Frank, to the scheme finally removed it from practical politics. After the fall of France in June 1940, the foreign office designed a new solution on the same lines, consisting of the removal of three to four million Jews to the island of Madagascar, which the French would cede to Germany. It would really be a penal settlement, ensuring the "good behavior" of American Jewry, with a hint that they might ransom their fellow Jews from captivity.[10] This was taken seriously enough until October 1940 to cause the Germans to expel some of the West German Jews into southern France, which would make sense only if this was a stage for the final removal of the Jews to a French colony.

We have no direct evidence at all as to when the mass murder policy was decided upon. Circumstantial evidence seems to point to the probability that it was Hitler himself who pushed his colleagues into the "Final Solution." As late as May 1940, Himmler wrote a memorandum for Hitler entitled "A Few Thoughts Regarding the Treatment of Alien-Nationals in the East," which won Hitler's approval. In it he advocated a policy of organized kidnapping of good-looking children of Slavic origins to Germany, coupled with deprivation of any kind of education for the Slavs, who would be reduced to slavery. He praised this method as the mildest and the best "when out of an inner conviction one rejects as un-German and impossible the bolshevist method of physical extermination of a people."[11] What apparently influenced Hitler's decision was the fact that he had given the orders to prepare for an attack on the Soviet Union (at the end of 1940), and he expected to find there a very large number of Jews—the Nazis thought that there were five million Jews in Russia (in fact there were about 3.5 million). The West obviously did not want his Jews, and an expulsion to an African island had become illusory in the light of British resistance to the Nazis. There was no longer any need to take Western opinion into consideration. Moreover, the future struggle with Russia was the great apocalyptic struggle for world dominance, in which the great adversary, lurking behind the Bolsheviks and the plutocrats alike, was World Jewry. The struggle would now be waged openly and with no holds barred. The background to Nazi antisemitism with its murderous dreams justified by the dehumanizing image of the Jew as the Devil now came into its own. It is really immaterial whether Hitler had had this at the back of his mind from 1938, or 1939, or 1940. He had not made any decisions regarding this problem, but now he and his followers must have seen the time as suddenly being just right for the physical destruction of real people who were both the symbol and the content of their concentrated fears, guilt complexes, and animosities. The decision was taken, most probably, in conjunction with a series of directives regarding the future treatment of civilian population in the areas about to be conquered in Russia. The date would have been around the Ides of March, 1941.

Implementation of the "Final Solution" began with the start of the Russian campaign, in June 1941. Four special murder groups (*Einsatzgruppen*), commanded in three out

of the four cases by members of the German intelligentsia,[12] began murdering the Jewish populations of the
newly conquered territories. Completely taken by surprise,
unprepared for the very thought of a systematic murder of
people without any apparent cause whatsoever, masses of
Jews were brutally assassinated. It is impossible to estimate their numbers; they vary in various accounts between one and two million, for the period up to the summer of 1942. Towards the end of the year, in December
1941, the first destruction machinery was set up in areas
outside of Russia, at Chelmno in the area annexed from
Poland in 1939. This must have been prepared weeks
previously at least, so that it is impossible to account for
the acceleration of the murder by the entry of the United
States into the war on 7 December 1941, with the Japanese attack on Pearl Harbor. We know now that Hitler
was as much taken by surprise with the Japanese attack as
anyone else, and Chelmno, where the Jews of the annexed
Warthegau were being gassed, was obviously quite uncon-
nected with general political developments.

In January 1942, a meeting in Berlin (the so-called
"Wannsee conference") took place of representatives of
various German ministries in order to coordinate the
murder actions. This has wrongly been represented as a
major turning point. In fact, it just was a meeting held for
purely administrative reasons to implement a decision that
had been taken about ten months previously and which
was in the process of being carried out. The decision of
Wannsee to "comb out" Europe's Jews from West to East
was not followed in any case; the first victims outside the
Russian sphere were in the Generalgouvernement (Central
Poland) where the Jewish populations of the Lublin district were sent to their deaths at the death camp of Belzec.
Other death camps soon came into operation in Poland—
Sobibor, Treblinka and Maidanek—and people not only

from Poland but also from other countries were shipped there. From early in 1942, Auschwitz became a center for the murder operations; if we are to believe its commander, Rudolf Hoess, he received Himmler's directives to establish Auschwitz as a killing center in the summer of 1941, well before the American entry into the war. In July 1942, Himmler ordered the destruction of Polish Jewry by the end of the year and the concentration of remaining working slaves, whose services could not be dispensed with temporarily, in a small number of concentration camps.

The main murder process took place between June 1941 and October 1942 for the occupied areas in Russia, between March 1942 (the destruction of the Lublin ghetto) and August 1943 (the destruction of the Bialystok ghetto) for Poland, between July 1942 and August 1943 for the western countries. The shock, the absolute unbelief, the tremendous speed, and the deception practiced—especially in the West—made a Jewish reaction both in Europe itself and outside it very difficult. By the summer of 1943, there were only remnants left of Jewish communities in the East, mainly in a few camps and in the ghetto of Lodz, which still had some 70,000 inhabitants. Of the three million Polish Jews in 1939 who had been caught in the Nazi trap, only some 300,000 were still alive. German Jewry and Dutch Jewry had been practically destroyed. Some 20,000 Jews were still alive in Slovakia, and in Belgium and France a majority of Jews were in hiding or leading a semi-legal existence. In Romania, Jews had been deported from the districts reconquered from the Russians early in the war, in June and July 1941, but the rest, there and in Hungary and in Bulgaria, were still alive, despite some terrible pogroms in Romania and the deportation to Poland of the Jews of Thrace and Macedonia. Remnants still existed in Croatia; in Italian-controlled areas Jews were protected, paradoxically, by Germany's Fascist allies.

Because of the sheer impossibility of a sudden and complete destruction as well as economic considerations, the murder of Jewish communities, especially in the East, usually took place in two stages. First came the mass deportation of the majority of the population; those who were left were then used for the German war effort, until they too were murdered. This policy gave the Jews that remained alive after the first mass deportation the possibility of reaction based on a realistic appreciation of what was awaiting them. All ghetto rebellions without exception took place after the mass deportation of the first stage—it could indeed hardly be any different. The ghetto rebellions of Warsaw (April–September 1943), Bialystok (August 1943), and the armed actions in some forty other ghettos took place among the remnants of Jewish populations. Armed action was widespread; in the areas of Belorussia some twenty-five thousand Jews escaped into the forests to fight the Germans, largely motivated by a burning desire for revenge. About two thousand Jewish partisans fought in the areas of central Poland, close to one thousand in the Warsaw ghetto, and in August and October 1943, rebellions took place in Sobibor and Treblinka death camps that effectively put these death camps out of action.[13]

It took quite some time before the Jews, even those in the areas first affected, realized what was happening to them. Ghettos were hermetically shut off from each other; surrounding populations, especially of Baltics and Poles, were either indifferent or actively hostile, with some notable and heroic exceptions. Communications between ghettos were very difficult and hazardous. Rumors were unbelievable and therefore not believed. Thus it took until the winter of 1941–42 before the population of Vilna ghetto came to believe the rumors that tens of thousands of their kith and kin had been murdered just a few miles outside Vilna in the woods of Ponary. A survivor of Chelmno who appeared in the Warsaw ghetto about February 1942 was not believed, nor were emissaries who came there from Vilna about the same time. It was not until the summer of 1942 that Jews generally began to realize that they were faced with total physical annihilation—that is, the survivors realized that; the majority of Polish Jews were no longer alive by then. In the West this process of awakening came much later, for most people probably only after liberation.

Any rescue action from the outside had to overcome these handicaps first. The process of knowing usually came in a number of stages: first, the information had to be disseminated; then, it had to be believed; then, it had to be internalized, that is, some connection had to be established between the new reality and a possible course of action; finally, there came action, if and when action came.

This process was also decisively influenced by the real power—or rather lack of it—of the Jews of the West. The essential difference between the position of the Jews in the two world wars was that in the first, Jews had some bargaining strength because they could choose between the two warring camps, although they were a small minority with doubtful influence; in the second, they suffered from an absolute powerlessness: they were in no position to choose between the warring sides (as the Arabs, for instance, were—and did), had no armed force of any value they could offer, and proved to be quite uninfluential from an internal political point of view. They could only appeal to the conscience of the democratic or Soviet world fighting against the Nazis, and while such a conscience did exist, it proved not to be powerful enough as a political factor to influence decisions of a practical nature. The powerlessness of the Jews inside the Nazi world was therefore matched by their powerlessness outside it. This fact was hard to accept, and most difficult to understand for the tormented Jews of Nazi Europe.

How much and what did Jewish leaders in New York or London know? When did they realize what it was that was happening to European Jews? How did they react to the knowledge thus obtained?

As far as the actual information was concerned, there can be no doubt at all that whoever read the papers, listened to the radio, or read the Jewish Telegraphic Agency's daily reports could have had all the information about Europe's Jews that was needed to establish the facts about the mass murder. We already know that information did not mean knowledge, but the information at any rate was there. In England, the *Jewish Chronicle* and the *Zionist Review* knew of Soviet reports regarding the massacres of Jews and other Soviet citizens—as it was usually put—early in 1942. The Jewish Telegraphic Agency, which was received in New York, originated some of these reports and hammered away at them. Yiddish papers, and later non-Jewish papers as well, brought accounts of mass murders in Vilna as early as March 1942.

Until June 1942, all this information was admittedly scattered. Nobody imagined a campaign of planned mass annihilation, and the information was always presented in a form that allowed for doubts as to its veracity. Yet even so, an article like that reporting Dr. Henry Shoskes's information regarding the Warsaw ghetto, which appeared in the *New York Times* on 1 March 1942, should have made people stop and think. Shoskes was well known and well thought of among American Jewish groups, and he stated that on the basis of reliable information he had,

"there will be no more Jews in Poland in five or six years."
This and many similar items of news were regarded sometimes as good propaganda, sometimes as exaggerations
that might unfortunately have some grain of truth in
them. In either case, while they indicated troubles and
loss of life, they did not in essence go beyond the very
harsh experiences of World War I.

The first authoritative and exact report on a general plan
to annihilate Polish Jewry was dated May 1942, and was
sent by the Bund (the Jewish Socialist Party of Poland,
which was anti-Zionist, anti-Communist, and advocated
Jewish cultural autonomy within a Socialist Poland). It
declared that the Germans had "embarked on the physical
extermination of the Jewish population on Polish soil." It
correctly related how the destruction process spread from
the east to western Poland and from there to the Generalgouvernement. It estimated the number of murdered
Jews at 700,000—rather an understatement.[14]

On 2 June 1942, the BBC broadcast the gist of this
report to Europe. The Polish National Council of the Polish government-in-exile in London issued a call to all
Allied parliaments, which included the main points of the
Bund report, on 10 June. This was repeated on 8 July,
and a note incorporating the main points was handed to
the American ambassador by the Poles in exile. A press
conference on 9 July was held to broadcast the contents of
the Bund report, at which the British Minister of Information, Brendan Bracken, and the Polish Minister for Home
Affairs, Stanislaw Mikolajczyk, participated along with
Jewish representatives. The *Daily Telegraph* carried the
report on 25 June, and then repeatedly referred to it during the following week. The Jewish Telegraphic Agency
carried all these items to America. Roman Catholic Cardinal Hinsley of London broadcast the information on 7

July, and the *Times* carried a garbled version of the 9 July press conference on 10 July.

Jewish organizations were informed of all this. They simply did not grasp what the information meant. The Zionists had held a conference at the New York Biltmore Hotel in May 1942 proclaiming the need for a Jewish state in the whole of Palestine to absorb all the millions of uprooted Jews from Europe. This plan was then adopted in Jerusalem by the Zionist Executive Council in November, after it had become well established that the millions were no more.

The publication of the Bund report, in England and in the United States, was met with both disbelief and shock. One gains the impression of total misunderstanding of the import of the information. Prompted by its two Jewish members, Szmul Zygielbojm and Ignacy Szwarcbart, the Polish National Council in London submitted another resolution on the massacre of the Jews to the Allied parliaments. A Polish White Book containing the information was circulated on 27 June. The Jewish Telegraphic Agency and the Jewish press carried information regarding the mass murders, especially those in the Baltic countries (which had taken place in 1941, but were only now reported).

Zionist papers in the United States reacted by stating that "the obvious aim of the Nazis is to bring about the destruction of the Jews," only to indicate subsequently that life for the Jews in Polish ghettos was going on.[15] Bundist publications were no different. *The Ghetto Speaks,* a periodical published in English for the specific purpose of disseminating information about Poland, stated on 1 August that "the Jewish nation in Poland is being ruthlessly annihilated." In the very next sentence it declared, "Jewish life continues now behind the ghetto walls."[16] A mass meeting in Madison Square Garden in mid-July 1942 protested the slaughter of the Jewish population in Nazi-occupied Europe. People were aware that something terrible was going on, did not dare to disbelieve openly, but could not bring themselves to lend credence to information that the total Jewish population of Nazi Europe was being murdered. The reason for this is not really difficult to understand. Jews were being killed in Europe for no other reason than that they had been born Jews (by Nazi definitions). The crime they were being accused of was one that quite literally had no precedent: they were accused of living, of having been born. This was stated repeatedly and openly in Nazi orders, regulations, etc., where "criminals" were accused of various transgressions; when it came to Jews, it was simply stated that they had been killed or punished because they were Jews. Raised and educated in an American society based on certain elemental values that ultimately derived from Jewish moral concepts, American Jews were singularly unprepared to adapt quickly to the thought that they were living in a different century from the one they had imagined.

On 8 August 1942, Dr. Gerhardt Riegner, the World Jewish Congress's representative at Geneva, sent off a cable which has commonly been interpreted as breaking the silence regarding the mass murder of European Jews. Yet a cursory perusal of the cable makes it clear that Riegner himself was very unsure what his information actually was. The cable said that Riegner had received "alarming report that in Fuhrer's headquarters plan discussed and under consideration" that all of Europe's Jews should be concentrated in the East and there "exterminated at one blow." The action was being planned for autumn and methods under discussion included "prussic acid." Riegner added, however, that he was transmitting the information "with all necessary reservation as exactitude cannot be confirmed." It is hardly surprising that the Americans should have had their doubts regarding reports that in Riegner's own eyes looked incredible; they decided not to hand the cable to Stephen S. Wise, as Riegner had requested, until the reports had been checked. On 28 August, however, Wise received the information from Sidney Silverman, head of the World Jewish Congress's London branch, because Riegner had sent a copy of his cable to London. Wise agreed not to make the information public; this, too, was a logical step to take, considering the fact that he had not acted upon the much more detailed and unequivocal Bund report two months before that.[17]

What happened between August and November in Switzerland, where Paul C. Squire of the American embassy was trying to find out whether Riegner's information had been correct, has been described in some detail in Arthur D. Morse's book *While Six Million Died.*[18] What apparently convinced the Americans more than anything else was the testimony of Dr. Carl J. Burckhardt, former League of Nations commissioner in Danzig and now the most active personality in the International Red Cross. Squire interviewed Burckhardt on 7 November 1942 and was told that Hitler had signed an order early in 1941 that before the end of 1942 Germany must be free of all Jews. Burckhardt added that the term *Judenfrei* as employed by his sources meant "extermination."[19]

In the meantime, the Poles in London also continued to receive this kind of unbelievable material. From time to time they made this information available to the British and American ambassadors to their government-in-exile, but no action seemed to result. As early as July, they had asked themselves, if "Polish informations from the Homeland {i.e., Poland] are not believed by the Anglo-Saxon nations because of their unlikeliness, surely they must believe their Jewish informants."[20] Poles, and even British, still believed in the great influence of Jews in America. But it was not until the Polish government submitted an official note on 9 December 1942 that the Allied nations finally undertook at least a symbolic act: on 17 December 1942 they published a condemnation of the massacre of the Jews, thus announcing officially that the Jews were actually being killed.[21] Parallel to this, the arrival in Palestine on 13 November 1942 of sixty-nine Jewish civilians who had been exchanged for Germans because they held Palestinian passports confirmed the information to Palestinian Jewry. From then on, information was published in great detail everywhere in the Allied world. Whether it was now believed is a different matter again.

What is decisive is the extent to which the information regarding the Holocaust became a guide to action. The change that came at the end of 1942 was not in the quality of the information, but lay in the fact that the Allies had now officially admitted the information to have been correct. Yet we find in the expressions and the actions of American Jewry a mixture of incredulity, hope that this might turn out to be a nightmare from which the Jewish people might one day mercifully wake up, utter despair resulting from an accurate appreciation of what was happening, a desire for immediate action, a terrible feeling of helplessness, and even a desire to escape responsibility and hide behind words or meaningless action. Typical perhaps of the muddle and disorientation of all sections of Jewry in the "Free World" was the declaration of the Bund in America, in October 1943, that "the common sufferings in the present Nazi Hell and the common fight of the Polish and Jewish underground Labor Movements will, certainly, strengthen the more the common bond of fate and struggle linking the Polish and Jewish masses."[22] *The Ghetto Speaks,* the publication that carried this declaration, had itself told its readers throughout the preceding year that only a few Jews were still left alive in Poland. Zionists, including leaders of the World Jewish Congress, were absorbed in postwar planning and were paying little more than ceremonial attention to what was happening in Europe—this, by the way, in direct contrast to their friends in Istanbul, whose letters and cables were one big outcry demanding immediate action to save the remnants.[23]

Thinking in terms of millions was a way for many people to escape the reality of murder of countless individual human beings, a way in which sanity could be preserved in the midst of unthinkable disaster. In Istanbul and in Geneva, Jewish representatives, whether of the Jewish Agency or of others, were closer to reality and could not understand why those in Palestine, or England, or America did not comprehend, and did not act in desperation and radically. Even there it took time before the reality sank in; when it did, letters were written that should have, and yet could not have, aroused Jews in the "Free World" to feverish activity. Istanbul reported letters from Nazi Europe, "their content—tears, and suffering, and despair, and madness and blood—much Jewish blood that will scream and boil and froth for thousands of years because it was spilt in vain."[24] Palestine Jewry did not understand this kind of language; American Jews would have to undergo a whole process of redefinition and rethinking before this became comprehensible at all.

American Jewry was hoping for results from the Bermuda conference, called in early 1943 ostensibly to find some solution to the "refugee question." In fact, the British and American governments were trying to find a way of appeasing public opinion which, especially in England, was demanding action to save not the refugees who had managed to escape to Spain or Switzerland, but the persecuted Jews of Europe. No nongovernmental agencies were permitted to participate at the meeting, opened at Bermuda on 19 April 1943 (the very day when the Warsaw ghetto rebellion began). American Jews followed the proceedings with great interest, and the reports to the British House of Commons and the debate that followed were carefully read in New York. It became clear that in the Allied view "these people" were "for the present mostly beyond the possibility of rescue. . . . We must, I think, recognise that the United Nations can do little or nothing in the immediate present for the vast numbers now under Hitler's control." So said Osbert Peake, British Under-Secretary for the Home Department on 15 May 1943, in the Commons. The line that was taken by Britain and America, and accepted by most Jews at the time, was that there was really nothing one could do to help Jews under Nazi rule, except to win the war quickly and save whatever could be saved that way. As a result, nothing that might hamper the war effort, including any rescue plan that diverted means and manpower from the pursuit of victory, could be justified. Occasionally, Jewish leaders might demand immediate action to rescue European Jewry—as for instance Henry Monsky did in his address at the American Jewish Conference on 29 August 1943. But this was more in the nature of lip service—he then went on to talk about postwar reconstruction. There were a few, but not many, who actually believed something could be done immediately to help. Only the lonely people in Istanbul and Geneva seem to have realized what opportunities were being missed: "it is not known in Palestine and perhaps they don't believe that it is still possible to help. The news that came from Geneva [i.e., the Riegner informations] did not convince; and just as before the mind could not grasp that this is how they are murdering us, so now the mind doesn't grasp that there are nooks and paths through which help can be given."[25] Even there, though, despair soon took hold. The Allies would not budge; there was no money; there was nothing one could really do. "On the whole I think that one can hardly do anything to extend help in the most crucial areas and all we are really doing is patchwork," wrote Richard Lichtheim, the Jewish Agency man in Geneva.[26]

The Bermuda conference ended with the decision to reactivate the Intergovernmental Committee for Refugees and open a camp in North Africa for those refugees who had managed to escape to Spain. This might open the way for some more refugees to cross the border. Beyond that, nothing was decided upon—or, more correctly, it was decided that nothing could and nothing should be done. The problem was not only Jewish, but that of other persecutees. They could not be helped anyway. No ships would be set apart to save them, no food would be allowed into Europe, no negotiations regarding civilians would be allowed to take place with Germany. No warning to Nazis and their collaborators was issued, no approaches were made to the Vatican, no guarantees for the upkeep of refugees and their care after the war were given to neutrals. Moreover, all the negative decisions were left unannounced and secret, while hope was held out for a time that more positive decisions had been reached.

Jewish organizations in America were, on the whole, fairly well informed regarding the lack of action taken at Bermuda. But in addition to the formidable psychological hindrances hinted at already there were certain objective circumstances that militated against any action that could have been described as "radical"—demonstrations, hunger strikes, and the like. Any such actions would have had to be taken against the Roosevelt administration, that very same government that had stood, for all its shortcomings, between the Jews and American antisemitism, which had been so very strong until 1942 at least. In 1942 the war was not going well. Any demonstration against the government was in fact a demonstration against the war. Demonstrate against Roosevelt?

Of course, with hindsight it is possible to take exception to this description, which is not to say that hindsight is necessarily invalid. Action was attempted, and might have been perhaps more successful if more representative groups had joined. Thus the mission in the United States of the Palestine Jewish rightist armed underground (the Irgun Zva'i Le'umi) managed to organize an Emergency Rescue Committee which roped in senators and congressmen and demanded action.

Slowly, as 1943 came to an end and 1944 arrived, the tragedy was accepted as fact—not really grasped, not really understood, but accepted as a kind of verdict from which one would have to restart life. There was a job to be done. Those who could be helped had to be helped; those who had to move had to be moved. Hungry people had to be fed. Jews who survived had to be assisted in their migrations. On 15 November 1943 the Jewish National Committee in underground Warsaw sent a message to London which said that "the blood of three million [Polish] Jews will cry out for revenge not only against the Hitlerite beasts, but also against the indifferent groups that, words apart, did not do anything to rescue the nation that was sentenced to destruction by the Hitlerite murderers."[27] And in the autumn of 1944, Ben Gurion wrote an article called "Before the Tribunal of History," in which he asked:

What have you done to us, you freedom-loving peoples, guardians of justice, defenders of the high principles of democracy and of the brotherhood of man? What have you allowed to be perpetrated against a defenceless people while you stood aside and let it bleed to death, without offering help or succour, without calling on the fiends to stop, in the language of retribution which alone they would understand. Why do you profane our pain and wrath with empty expressions of sympathy which ring like a mockery in the ears of millions of the damned in the torture house of Nazi Europe? Why have you not even supplied arms to our ghetto rebels, as you have done for the partisans and underground fighters of other nations? Why did you not help us to establish contacts with them, as you have done in the case of the partisans in Greece and Yugoslavia and the underground movements elsewhere? If, instead of Jews, thousands of English, American or Russian women, children and aged had been tortured every day, burnt to death, asphyxiated in gas chambers—would you have acted in the same way?[28]

That was the context within which we shall try to discuss some questions regarding the Holocaust.

2. Against Mystification: The Holocaust as a Historical Phenomenon

TO MYSTIFY: TO MAKE OBSCURE OR SECRET. THAT is how a dictionary defines the term.[1] Of late, the Holocaust has been subjected to a great deal of treatment resulting in obscurity or obfuscation. This should not really surprise us. The event is of such a tremendous magnitude that an ordinary person's mind is incapable of absorbing it. There will therefore be a natural tendency to run away from it, deny it, and, mainly, try to reduce it to shapes and sizes that we can cope with, reaching back into our own experience. This of course applies to those attempts at mystification that are not motivated by ulterior purposes. People whose political or ideological predilections are anti-Jewish will produce denials or obfuscations that are in accord with their prejudices. The line between "authentic" and "unauthentic" responses, as Emil Fackenheim termed them,[2] is sometimes rather thin. The purpose of this chapter is to try to examine some such mystifications.

The first of these arises out of the misuse of the term Holocaust, but it is not just a semantic argument. The problem posed is: What do you mean when you say Holocaust? The term, whether appropriate or not, has come to be used for the mass murder of probably around 5.8 million Jewish people in Europe under the Nazi regime.[3] This, to some of us, may sound a trite sort of statement. Is it not clear that this is what we mean by it? Well, no, not exactly. In October 1977, when the New York Board of Education discussed a curriculum on the Holocaust to be introduced into the public education of the city, letters were written to the *New York Times* indicating that the Holocaust was much wider than just the murder of the Jews. It was pointed out that Poles, Lithuanians, and others were also murdered, and after the war the Soviets engaged in wholesale destruction of, for instance, the Baltic nationalities.[4] "Holocaust" has been widely used to describe the discrimination against Blacks in the United States, against Jews in the U.S.S.R., against Arabs in Israel's occupied territories, and against any number of other victims of real or imagined injustices perpetrated all over the globe.

The term Holocaust, as Gerd Korman pointed out in an article some years ago,[5] came into use in the English language to describe what happened to European Jews only some years after the end of World War II, between 1957 and 1959. The feeling was widespread that what had happened to the Jews was in some way unique, or unprecedented or, as Roy Eckardt put it, "uniquely unique."[6] Yet here we are faced with a very real problem: if what happened to the Jews was unique, then it took place outside of history, and it becomes a mysterious event, an upside-down miracle, so to speak, an event of religious significance in the sense that it is not man-made as that term is normally understood. On the other hand, if it is not unique at all, then where are the parallels or the precedents?

In order to avoid mystification, we must therefore probe the historical backgroud. The uniqueness of the position of Jews in the Nazi world was that they had been singled out for total destruction. Not because of their views or their religion, their age or their sex, but simply because they had been born of three Jewish grandparents. In other words, for the first time in history a sentence of death had been pronounced on anyone guilty of having been born, and born of certain parents. The only way of avoiding that death sentence was not to have been born of three Jewish grandparents—a patent absurdity. This Nazi decision was based on an ideology in which the Jew was defined as the anti-race, or in other words as that mixture of characteristics that could be described, in Nazi terms, as an absolute evil. Leaning very heavily on Christian theology, but twisting it in accordance with their own ideas, the Nazis made the Jew the Satan to their Christ, who was Hitler.[7] The Jew was the personification of evil, and thus not human at all. He only appeared human, and when the Nazis had to describe what the Jew was in their eyes, they borrowed terms from the insect world that aroused feelings of disgust—cockroaches, parasites—or from the microbe world—viruses, and so on.[8] The Jew then was both a devil and a parasite. The devilish quality of the Jew expressed itself in his desire to rule the world and to destroy the healthy, Nordic races by biological and cultural corruption. Just like the medieval image of the devil, the Nazi image of the Jewish devil had very marked sexual overtones. The chief way in which the Jew corrupted the Aryan nations was through intermarriage and sexual contact generally. The blood of the Gentile was contaminated, hopelessly corrupted, by even one such contact, and this contamination was hereditary. The Jews had a world government, hiding behind their religious and other organizations, and this government was out to rule and destroy.

This picture agreed with the notorious "Protocols of the Elders of Zion," a forgery produced by the Tsarist police in 1905, purporting to describe a meeting supposedly held at the founding of the Zionist movement in 1897. There, the forgery said, the Jews had prepared their plans to control the world.[9] The Nazis complemented this picture by arguing that as the Jews were parasites and incapable of either a productive life or a permanent political structure of their own, they would, like any other parasite, destroy not only their victim, but in the end themselves as well, because they could never exist on their own.

The result of this pernicious fantasy, which was believed by many thousands of the Nazi party's ardent adherents, was that the ground was prepared for doing away with the Jews, if the occasion arose. For if the Jew was the incarnation of the Devil, or the Devil himself, or if he was the implacable enemy of the Nordic races, out to control the world, or if he was not really human but a kind of dangerous parasite, then the normal laws of human behavior did not apply to his treatment by the Nazis. The Nazis did not treat the Jews as humans because they did not see them as humans.[10]

The problem arises, what was the Nazis' attitude to other groups, to Slavs, for instance. There are any number of textbook or lay statements that the Nazis began their destruction with the Jews, and had the Nazi regime persisted for any length of time, Poles, Czechs, Russians, and others would have suffered the same fate. There is some basis in fact for this statement. It is not definitely known how many Soviet prisoners of war were killed by the Nazis through starvation and ill-treatment, but they cannot have been less than two and a half million.[11] There were many thousands of Polish intelligentsia who were murdered by the Nazis during the first year of occupation in Poland in a special "drive." Tens of thousands of other Poles were brutally murdered as resistants, real or imagined. Whole Polish villages were destroyed.[12] The Czech intelligentsia were treated only very slightly better. At Lidice, all males were indiscriminately butchered. Many thousands of Russian, Belorussian, and Ukrainian peasants were slaughtered during the German occupation.

The purposes and aims of these policies were clearly defined in a memorandum submitted by Himmler to Hitler in May 1940.[13] They were designed to denationalize the East European nations, absorb into the Germanic race those people who were of what the Nazis thought was "Nordic" blood, murder the intelligentsia, destroy all autochthonous cultural life, and turn the rest into a mass of slave laborers who would enjoy the benefits of the Nazi Kultur by building its monuments and continuing to exist under the strict but just rule of their overseers. What emerges from a detailed examination of both the theory and the practice is a policy of selective murder designed to destroy the nations as such, but keep most of their members alive to become a Helot working force for the glory of the Reich.

What shall we call this policy? We could do worse than quote the man who invented the term "genocide," Raphael Lemkin. Writing in 1943, and referring to the German policy in occupied Europe, he said:

The practice of extermination of nations and ethnic groups as carried out by the invaders is called by the author "genocide." . . . Genocide is effected through a synchronized attack on different aspects of life of the captive peoples: in the political field (by destroying institutions of self-government and imposing a German pattern of administration, and through colonization by Germans); in the social field (by disrupting the social cohesion of the nation involved and killing or removing elements such as the intelligentsia, which provide spiritual leadership . . .); in the cultural field (by prohibiting or destroying cultural institutions and cultural activities; by substituting vocational education for education in the liberal arts, in order to prevent humanistic thinking . . .); in the economic field (by shifting the wealth to Germans . . .); in the biological field (by a policy of depopulation and by promoting procreation by Germans in the occupied countries); in the field of physical existence (by introducing a starvation rationing system for non-Germans and by mass killings, mainly of Jews, Poles, Slovenes, and Russians); in the religious field (by interfering with the activities of the Church, which in many countries provides not only spiritual but also national leadership); in the field of morality (by attempts to create an atmosphere of moral debasement through promoting pornographic publications and motion pictures, and the excessive consumption of alcohol).[14]

The lengthy quote is, I think, appropriate, because this definition of the term "genocide" has been universally accepted. Clearly, what was happening to quite a number of peoples in Nazi Europe was genocide: their institutions of learning closed, their political leadership decimated, their language and national culture discarded, their churches eliminated from a free exercise of their functions, their wealth despoiled, and subjected to killings of groups and individuals as the Nazis pleased—they were victims of the crime defined, or described, by Lemkin. The difference between that and the Holocaust lies in the difference between forcible, even murderous, denationalization, and wholesale, total murder of every one of the members of a community. Contrary to legend, there never was a Nazi policy to apply the measures used against the Jews to other national communities. It was quite natural for the commander of the Polish underground Home Army, General Stefan Rowecki (Grot), to publish, on 10 November 1942, an order to his organization referring to the "extermination of the Jews" and the fear of the "Polish society, that after the termination of this action, the Germans will commence to liquidate the Poles in the same manner" ("że po zakończeniu tej akcji Niemcy zaczną w ten sposób likwidować Polaków.").[15] When the Polish rebellion of August-September 1944 collapsed and the Polish inhabitants of Warsaw were expelled from the ruined city, many Poles thought that they would now suffer the fate of the

Jews. But there was a vast difference between the subjective feeling of the threatened populace and the actual plans and policies pursued by the oppressors. The only group that was destined for wholesale murder was the Jews, for the reasons we have outlined above. From what we know of the Nazi policy towards the Gypsies, a parallel exists, but it is more apparent than real. There were Gypsy tribes that were murdered, and there were others that were protected. Individual Gypsies living among the rest of the population were not ferreted out and many even served in the Nazi army. It appears that the Nazis were ambivalent about what to do with them, but those who were murdered were the victims more of a campaign against so-called "asocials" than against the Gypsy people as such.

To sum up, there may be no difference between Holocaust and genocide for the victim of either. But there are gradations of evil, unfortunately. Holocaust was the policy of the total, sacral Nazi act of mass murder of all Jews they could lay hands on. Genocide was horrible enough, but it did not entail *total* murder if only because the subject peoples were needed as slaves. They were, indeed, "subhumans" in Nazi terminology. The Jews were not human at all.

Not to see the difference between the concepts, not to realize that the Jewish situation was unique, is to mystify history. On the other hand, to declare that there are no parallels, and that the whole phenomenon is inexplicable, is equally a mystification. The partial similarity to the Gypsies has been mentioned already. During World War I, about half of the Armenian population in Anatolia was murdered by Enver Pasha's troops. Yet at the same time, the Armenians at Istanbul, the heart of the Ottoman Empire, were not killed. The Armenian massacres are indeed the closest parallel to the Holocaust; they were motivated largely by extreme nationalism and religious fanaticism, and were not total—whereas the Nazi policy towards the Jews was motivated by a pseudoreligious and anti-Christian ideology that was based on a very deep antisemitic European tradition, and it was total and logical. The differences are as important as the parallels are.

In the post-Holocaust world there have been several genocides and several near-Holocausts already. Suffice it to mention the threatened mass murder of the pro-Indian Bihari minority in Bangladesh during the struggle for independence of that country, the horrible fate of the Kurds in contemporary Iraq, the threatened slaughter of the Christian population in Lebanon, or the fate of Sudanese Blacks, the so-called Anya-Anya, over two million of whom are said to have perished in a number of punitive expeditions organized by the central Sudanese government.

There is of course no unique event in history, beyond the trite statement that every event is nonrepeatable. Once an event has happened, it can happen again, not in precisely the same form, but in one of an infinite number of variations. Events happen because they are possible. If they were possible once, they are possible again. In that sense, the Holocaust is not unique, but a warning for the future. I prefer to use Emil Fackenheim's term "epoch-making event" for the Holocaust.[16] It is as if we viewed a forbidding landscape of dark, deadly sheer rocks and bare mountains, in whose middle there rises a huge volcano spouting forth fire and lava. The volcano becomes meaningless if viewed without the natural background from which it rises. To view the landscape without the volcano is equally a denial of reality. To view the Holocaust as just another case of man's inhumanity to man, to equate it with every and any injustice committed on this earth— and, God knows, the number is endless—to say that the Holocaust is the total of all the crimes committed by

Nazism in Europe, to do any or all of this is an inexcusable abomination based on the mystification of the event. On the other hand, to view it as totally unique is to take it out of history and out of the context of our everyday lives, and that means opening wide the gates for a possible repetition.

We should properly use the term "Holocaust" to describe the policy of total physical annihilation of a nation or a people. To date, this has happened once, to the Jews under Nazism.

Let me now very briefly deal with another form of mystification which I find most disturbing. This arises out of a recent trend in historiography which, a generation after the event, is trying to deny some of the basic facts. There are two distinctive groups of writings or actions connected with this. One of them is the neo-Nazi gutter history; the other is a well-respected, seemingly serious attempt to question accepted visions of the Nazi period.

The Nazi gutter historiography not only exists, but flourishes. A French postwar convert to Nazism, Paul Rassinier, started the fashion with his book *Le Mensonge d'Ulysse* (Paris, 1955).[17] He was not sure whether gassing installations existed at Auschwitz. It was clear, to him in any case, that the Jews invented the story about their murder. Two German Nazis, Heinz Roth and Manfred Roeder, have been writing pamphlets and booklets repeating the canard.[18] The United Nations have had read into the protocol of the General Assembly a speech by His Excellency the delegate from Saudi Arabia, Jamil Baroody, on 24 and 25 March 1976,[19] which explicitly denied that the Holocaust ever happened. Baroody quoted from Rassinier and the others. Recently, in New York, a self-styled representative of the German-American community, Georg Pape, repeated the same argument.[20] One could

dismiss this as a passing *Schweinerei,* but this kind of propaganda has received considerable support from a book
recently published by a professor of electrical engineering
at Northwestern University,[21] who tries to prove that the
Jews were not murdered—well, one million maybe died in
the war, just as many millions of others did, but all the
rest fled to the Soviet Union, where they were absorbed by
the Communists, and the rest immigrated to the United
States and Israel. The Soviets did not report this, but then
you cannot rely on Communist statistics. There were no
gassing installations at Auschwitz—or, rather, the installations there were designed for the disinfection of
clothes because of the typhoid epidemics, but no humans
were gassed. The Jews were transported to the East, just as
the Germans claimed. Faced with the evidence of the Nazi
murderers themselves, this Nazi book simply says they
testified under pressure, or else the testimonies are
forgeries.

One really should add to the gutter literature the prod-
ucts that come out of Eastern Europe and the Soviet
Union, and that claim that the Zionists collaborated with
the Nazis in killing off the Jewish masses. There are too
many examples to quote from, but let me mention just a
certain Jiří Bohátka, who writes for the Czech press, and
who specializes in distributing this kind of poison.[22] In
Poland today, the fact that the Warsaw ghetto rebellion
was led by Zionists, as were the ghetto rebellions in Bialystok, Cracow, Czestochowa, Tarnow, and other places,
is not mentioned at all. More than that: no mention is
made of the fact that these were Jewish rebellions—in contemporary Polish literature these are said to have been
resistance acts by the Polish population, believe it or not.

Why is this literature so appealing and so dangerous?
Why is it copied and used by opponents of Israel, such as
Dr. Mehdi of the Arab-American group, who explicitly

used it in a recent communication quoted in the *New York Times?* [23] There is a basis of antisemitism pervading what we know as Western culture. For a certain time the facts of the Holocaust made antisemitism a phenomenon that was beyond the pale for civilized humans. But a generation after the event the old poison reasserts itself, especially when you consider that the facts of the Holocaust are indeed unbelievable. Why on earth should a modern technological society at war devote some of its very scarce resources to murder potential laborers whom it desperately needs in its production plants? Has anyone ever heard of a regime that simply murders whole populations for no other reason but their grandparents' religious or ethnic background? The Jews that were led into the gas chambers had no idea what was happening to them in a majority of cases. It was unprecedented, impossible, contrary to all previous experience. Why should you, thirty years after, believe it? Just because it happens to be the truth? When you combine the tradition of Jew-hatred, so brilliantly analyzed just recently again by Franklin H. Littell in his book *The Crucifixion of the Jews,* [24] with the specific problems engendered by the Holocaust, you have the foundation for contemporary anti-Jewishness. When you add to it the fact that, contrary to Christian antisemitic doctrine and contrary to Communist doctrine, the Jewish people exercised their right to self-determination and reemerged into global political history after the Holocaust, then it is not surprising that literature designed to deny the whole background of contemporary Jewish life is written and is believed. If you deny or obscure the Holocaust, in part or in whole, you have created the necessary precondition for a denial of the right of the continued existence of the Jewish people in the post-Holocaust world.

Denial of the Holocaust can be made in a more refined way than in the openly Nazi literature. Thus, for instance, the recent best seller by David Irving, *Hitler's War*,[25] does not actually deny the mass murders themselves, though it refers to them only very briefly. Irving befogs the issue in another way. He claims that it was not Nazi Germany that was solely responsible for the Second World War. He presents Hitler as a perfectly normal human being, and he denies that Hitler knew anything about the murder of the Jews prior to 1943. He de-demonizes Hitler. The same tendency can be seen in Joachim Fest's famous film, now being shown all over Western Europe, in which the question is asked: How did Hitler seduce the German people? A one-sided treatment of the Hitler phenomenon tends to make a bagatelle of the basic immorality of the regime and hides its murderous quality. Explicitly, Fest declares that his is another attempt to de-demonize Hitler.[26]

The problem with this is that one cannot get away from the demonic, or totally evil, qualities of the Nazi regime. One cannot de-demonize Hitler, because Hitler *was* a totally evil personality operating within a framework that only very evil personalities could exist in. "Evil" here stands in basic contradiction to the Ten Commandments and their social, economic, religious, philosophical, and other consequences. Once one de-demonizes Hitler, contrary to all historic evidence, one can then come up with the ultimate absurdity of denying that the dictator of the Third Reich knew anything about the way the Jews were dealt with, which is what David Irving says. By implication one then denies the main point in Hitler's whole program. But Hitler's war of conquest was ideologically a war against the Jews, as Lucy Dawidowicz rightly pointed out.[27] His attack on the Soviet Union was motivated by a struggle for *Lebensraum* of the Reich, and the real enemy was World Jewry, which, in its Bolshevik guise, was not only denying that *Lebensraum* to the Germanic peoples but was trying to establish a world rule of its own, albeit a parasitical world rule destined ultimately to self-destruction.

If you permit me to quote from Hitler's turgid prose, this will become clear: "Present-day Russia," he says,

has received as master the Jew, who first eliminated the former upper stratum and now must prove his own state-forming power. In view of the endowment of Jewry, which after all is only destructive, it will operate here only as the historical "ferment of decomposition." . . . A gigantic land area will thus be surrendered to the most variegated fate . . . and a period of the most restless changes will begin. . . . it is good fortune for the future that this development has taken place in just this way because thereby a spell has been broken which would have prevented us from seeking the goal of German policy there where it solely and exclusively can lie: territory in the East. . . . [The Jew] tries to bring nations into a state of unrest, to divert them from their true interests, and to plunge them into reciprocal wars and in this way gradually . . . rise to mastery over them. His ultimate goal is the denationalization, the promiscuous bastardization of other peoples, the lowering of the racial level of the highest peoples as well as the domination of this racial mishmash. . . . The end of the Jewish world struggle therefore will always be a bloody Bolshevization . . . hence the result of Jewish domination is always the ruin of all culture and finally the madness of the Jew himself.

The basic aim of Hitler was always the struggle against the Jews. To befog this issue is to misunderstand the whole historical process.[28]

The historians and journalists who write in a revisionist vein are by no means agreed on the angles of their critique of the older historiography. Irving denies the Nazi war guilt. Fest simply ignores the central problems and concentrates on marginal issues. Geoffrey Barraclough, one of the greatest living historians, goes a step further.[29] To him, the whole problem of the Nazi regime is secondary. Communism is important, the Third World is central. Nazism was a regrettable, brief episode, not really worth

wasting much time on. This is of course the final absurdity. You ignore the dozens of millions of dead of dozens
of nations, you ignore totally the vast destruction of cultural values and heritages, you ignore completely the totalitarian structure that spawned all this and the possible
paradigmatic quality of Nazism. You can then ignore the
Holocaust, or brush it aside as a footnote. Nazism taught
that the purpose of industry can be to produce death in
specially designed death factories—so what? Nazism
taught that you can combine an ancient hatred with modern technology and liquidate, or rather gassify, an ancient
people lock, stock, and barrel, and nobody in the so-called
free world will budge—so what? The credibility of Western civilization is called into question because, as Littell
pointed out, this was done by baptized Christians in the
midst of Christianity—so what? To Professor Barraclough,
this is a footnote. Our problem lies in the fact that the
revisionist intellectuals, from A. J. P. Taylor through Barraclough, Werner Maser, and Joachim Fest in Germany,
and the many others who lately seem to be jumping onto
this particular bandwagon, have created the preconditions
for a rehabilitation of Nazism and have thereby paved the
way for a linkup between revisionist history and neo-Nazi
pseudoscientific gutter history. It is by no means certain
that spreading the teaching of the Holocaust as wide and
as far as possible will successfully prevent any such un-
toward development; but we fight, therefore we are.

There is a third type of mystification to which I want to
address myself, consisting of two contradictory aspects.
On the one hand, we find a well-meant and perfectly legitimate allegorization and symbolization of the events of the
Holocaust, which may lead to the relegation of the Holocaust into mythology and empty universalization. And on
the other hand is the supposedly "scientific," "academic"

treatment of the Holocaust that turns the event into a vast sea of footnotes and rationalistic analyses, a subject matter for academic careers, doctoral theses, and suchlike, avoiding the abyss that was the Holocaust, turning the Holocaust into the subject of Holocaustology, a subbranch of history on equal footing with the study of the rise of the silk industry in France in the mercantilist era. In other words, we teach how to wipe out the Holocaust without having to shed a tear.

Let us turn to the first problem. Katzetnik (Yehiel Dinur) the great Holocaust novelist, whose works are, alas, not well known in the English-speaking world, writes books about Auschwitz. The books are written in a combination of naturalistic and symbolistic prose. But when he came to describe Auschwitz, he called it "Another Planet."[30] In his many writings and speeches, Elie Wiesel makes the point that the Holocaust was inexplicable, that the only true reaction to it would have been silence, that the problem posed by the Holocaust is man's relation to man and God, that in essence you cannot explain Auschwitz with a God and you cannot exclude God from Auschwitz. The contradictions in any approach to the problem of Auschwitz lead him to speak, but speak in pain. Not directly—except in his first novel, *The Night*—but symbolically, allegorically.

There is of course a sense in which there is absolutely no way by which one can approach the reality of Auschwitz. Not even the most trivial pain of one human can be actually felt by another human. It is only by a similar, or equivalent, experience that a person is prepared for an explanation or partial understanding of the other's experience. When, however, one approaches an event that is unprecedented, there are vast difficulties in making an understanding possible. The well-known and much-used Hassidic parable applies here: that the Ba'al Shem Tov knew the prayer that had to be said at an appointed time and an appointed place over a fire lit in the midst of a forest, a prayer that would be heard and would avert a calamity. And his disciple would know the time and the place, and how to light the fire, but he no longer knew the prayer. But that was enough, and the prayer of the heart was heard. And his disciple no longer knew the place in the forest, but there was a prayer in his heart. We who were not in that terrible forest of the Holocaust no longer have the ability fully to understand what transpired there, but we learn from the words of those who were there, though the words are but shadows. The symbols that we use are designed to make the event more understandable, more reachable. Were this not so, the Holocaust would die with the generation that went through it. The extreme insistence on the right of only the direct survivors of the Holocaust to describe it, deal with it, analyze it, and agonize about it, is in effect a death sentence on any understanding of that "epoch-making event." On the contrary, the crucial problem is how to anchor the Holocaust in the historical consciousness of the generations that follow it.

Were we to say that the Holocaust took place on another planet, we would in effect enable mankind to run away from it—what a marvelous, elegant form of escapism! It would then seem terrible, mysterious, far away, and not ours. If the problem is perceived as being primarily one of God's intervention, or of Satan's, then we do not have to bother about a historical understanding. Instead of the Nazis being responsible, an inexorable, mysterious, supernatural force caused this event. Human responsibility is removed from the scene, except in vague universalistic generalizations like "the results of prejudice," "man's inhumanity to man," and similar meaningless drivel.

The poets, the writers, the true mystics, the Katzetniks

and Wiesels and Schwarz-Barts, are as far from falling into this trap themselves as possible. They have not only experienced, they have learned and read. They know the factual background, the broad European framework, they have battled with historical and sociological analyses that certainly do not explain the deeper meanings, but without which no discoveries of such meanings appear possible.

What does one do, however, with students who come to a fifty-minute lecture about the Holocaust in general, having read two novels and one poem, who experience their emotional catharsis, and go away cleansed and purified, never to touch the subject again, not having learned a thing? The flow of words, even a flow of words about silence, hides an emptiness, a lack of realization of the here and now of the Holocaust, of its being a phenomenon not of the past but of the present. I fear we have to delve into the reality of the matter to be able to scale the emotional heights: what were the bases of Nazi Jew-hatred? What in Christian theology, in popular antisemitism, prepared the ground? Who were the murderers? What social strata did they come from? What did they think? When was the mass murder planned and how? How did the bureaucracy work that was able to sit behind their desks and direct the murder? Who built the gas chambers? What was the reaction of the victims? Sheep to the slaughter? Glorious resistance? Was there a way of rescue? What were the relations between Jew and non-Jew in the European countries occupied by the Nazis? What were the demographic, cultural, psychological consequences of the Holocaust? How did the State of Israel, into which two-thirds of the survivors immigrated, emerge just three years after the end of the mass murder? What are the effects of the Holocaust on the Jewish people, in Israel and in the Diaspora? What is the responsibility of the free world towards this event?

Such questions and many others cannot be avoided. It is only when they are faced that Katzetnik, Wiesel, Abba Kovner, Nelly Sachs, and the others become intelligble and meaningful. Without a return to the very hard and arduous task of actually knowing something about the Holocaust, the symbolic descriptions that occupy, quite legitimately, the center of the literary stage in Holocaust literature, become just another escape route for the superficial. Mass meetings with tears and emotion may be genuine; they may also be just another cheapening of the experience, or even a desecration of the memory of the victims.

The other way of mystification is that of which I myself may, heaven forbid, be guilty, and which I unwittingly may perpetuate in my students. It is the way of academization, of turning away from the abyss,[31] of escape by way of a footnote. In my own classes at the Hebrew University, I make my students go and see at least one Holocaust film during the year, lest they think they are dealing with a sterile, clean scientific enquiry. I can testify myself to the ease with which you can describe murder and then turn it into a seminar paper. There are hardly any easier ways to dehumanize the dead after their murder than by unconsciously imitating the Nazis and turning them into objects once again—this time objects of historical, sociological, or other research. To use once again Franklin Littell's terminology, the combination between Techne and Clio can indeed be deadly.

How then do we avoid mystification without destroying the mysterious quality that every historical event, and most certainly this one, possesses?

The first thing to remember is that the Holocaust was an actual occurrence in our century. It was not the product of an inexplicable fate or of a supernatural intervention, but one logical, possible outcome of European history. It was done by reasonably educated people in the midst of the most civilized continent on this earth, and, in fact, the ss, the murderers, were led by highly educated and sophisticated individuals. We must, I think, bear in mind that the ideology, the bureaucratic practice, and the psychology of the murderer have to be studied in order to advance to a better understanding of the event. The study of the victim and the bystander are of equal importance. The Jews were not passive victims: they tried to fight for their existence, without arms in most cases; they tried to survive, to escape, to run. They also tried to fight. The bystanders, both in Europe and in the non-Nazi world outside, acted and reacted, or remained passive. We must ask why and how. The story, its background, its consequences, must be told and taught. When doing that, we must be accurate and conscientious. All the footnotes must be right. All the documents must be genuine. Everything we say must be subject to the most rigorous known scientific verification processes. The responsibility we feel must try to be commensurate with the vastness of this "epoch-making event." I turn to those of you who happen to be Jewish. You are all the survivors of the Holocaust. It is only by accident that your parents, grandparents, or great-grandparents came here and did not stay there as their relatives did. You must find out who you are, where you come from, what the Jewish people lost in the gas chambers and the shooting pits. You must find out how *they* behaved and why. You are the descendants and heirs of a great civilization. Why did it happen to you? How did we face the most terrible thing any civilization has faced to date? What is the meaning of it to the Jewish people, and to others?

I turn to those of you who happen to be of non-Jewish parentage. It could have been you, or your parents. The Holocaust has created a precedent. Will it be followed? The non-Jewish governments, including that of the

United States, bear a sad share in the responsibility. You must learn so that a flicker of a chance may exist that we may avoid a repetition. Who can tell who the Jews will be next time?

We must be aware of the danger of the morass of footnoting. We must approach the Holocaust from both ends. The Jewish people were caught in a cage; they had no way out. The hopelessness of their situation, the problems they faced, their behavior in the face of death, all these cannot be relegated to our historical research alone. You cannot approach an understanding of the Holocaust without the soul-searing writings of those who were there and of those who learned from them. So we have to do both.

I would argue in favor of an alliance of the Chronicler with Job, as a way of approaching the problems of the Holocaust.

3. *Jew and Gentile:*
The Holocaust and After

THE PROBLEM UNDER DISCUSSION IS THE INTERRELA-
tionship of Jews and non-Jews during the Holocaust, and
the aftereffects of that relationship. It may perhaps surprise you, but it is, I think, correct to say that the overall
topic of Jewish-Gentile relationships during the Holocaust
has not been researched, except for certain areas or certain
incidents during the Holocaust. Thus, there have been any
number of comments on Polish-Jewish relationships during the war, and one of the first pieces of historical writing
on the Holocaust, coming out of the Holocaust itself, was
the great essay of Emmanuel Ringelblum, the historian of
the Warsaw ghetto, called "Polish-Jewish Relations during the Second World War," written in late 1943 and
early 1944, while Ringelblum was in hiding in a bunker
at 81 Grojecka Street in Warsaw.[1] Other postwar Jewish
writing emphasized some of the negative conclusions
regarding Polish attitudes toward Jews, and produced an
apologetic Polish response by one of those who tried to
save Jews during the war, Wladyslaw Bartoszewski, who
emphasized the rescue work done by Poles and Polish institutions under Nazi occupation.[2] But it is only now that
two of my colleagues at the Institute of Contemporary
Jewry and Yad Vashem are putting thousands of little
pieces together in an effort to go beyond the stage of ac-

cusations and apologetics, using innumerable memoirs and testimonies, including German, Polish, and Jewish documentation.[3]

Only in two other European countries has a comparable beginning been made: Denmark, where Leni Yahil's definitive study on *The Rescue of Danish Jewry* deals, among other things, in great detail with the attitude of the Danish people to their Jewish cocitizens, and Bulgaria, where Frederick Chary has written a first comprehensive account.[4]

Much more has been written concerning the contemporary attitudes of the free world to the Jews under Nazi rule. David S. Wyman, Henry L. Feingold, and Saul S. Friedman have dealt and are dealing with the attitude of the American government to the Jews under Nazi rule.[5] No comparable study exists for the British side, but there is research underway that should make clearer the attitude of the British government. First beginnings have been made regarding Soviet policies by some of my colleagues in Jerusalem, and the very important problem of the Polish government-in-exile will be at least partly dealt with in the study of Polish-Jewish relations referred to above. No studies have yet been made of the Czechoslovak and the West European governments-in-exile in London, or of the Latin American governments. There are some rather unsatisfactory studies of Swiss attitudes, basing themselves on an excellent but unfortunately almost unobtainable confidential study by the Swiss professor Carl Ludwig, prepared in 1957 for the Swiss government.[6] A brilliant study of the Spanish government's attitude appears in my colleague Haim Avni's recent book, soon to be published in English.[7] No studies have appeared on Sweden and Turkey.

In a sense, we can discuss the vast problem of Jewish-Gentile relationships while we are not yet burdened with too much knowledge—a very happy state of affairs in historical enquiry. At the same time we must try to go beyond that stage as far as we can. In order to do so, allow me briefly to deal with each of the major areas of discussion: the interrelationship in Nazi-occupied Europe, the attitudes of neutral countries, and the attitude of the Allied governments. In order to limit somewhat this already vast field, I will not deal at all with certain problems that should really belong to it, namely the relationships in concentration, labor, and death camps, and the attitudes of Jewish organizations in the free world.

Even a cursory glance at the available information makes it clear that one of the more important determinants of the fate of European Jewry during the Holocaust was the attitude towards them of their non-Jewish neighbors. Protection given to Jews by the peoples conquered by the Nazis was in many cases life-saving. Absence of such protection left the Jews to the mercies of the ss murderers and their collaborators from among the other European nations. We are therefore dealing not with a historical footnote, but with a central historical problem which, like many other such central problems, in the end boils down to a moral challenge: were the Gentiles their Jewish brothers' keepers?

It is impossible not to summarize at least the main emergent results of intermediate research on Eastern Europe, especially Poland. The Jews in prewar Poland were subject to a tremendous wave of Jew-hatred, which expressed itself in economic boycott and blatant discrimination, and in occasional pogroms. Polish political parties such as the National Democrats (Endeks, later the SN) [8] in opposition, and the government-controlled OZN (Oboz Zjednoczenia Narodowego) grouping, quite apart from the Fascist-oriented national radical youth organized in the ONR (Oboz Narodowo-Radykalny), saw in the expulsion of

the 3.3 million Jews from Poland one of the chief means
of Polish economic, social, and political regeneration. National socialist ideology undoubtedly influenced wide
strata of the Polish middle classes, at least on the Jewish
question. The peasants were less extreme, but certainly
not pro-Jewish. Even in the PPS, the Polish Socialist party
(Polska Partia Socjalistyczna), there were groups that were
not happy with the stand against antisemitism being taken
by some of their leaders.

The perennial economic crisis in Poland had a great deal
to do with the antisemitism rampant among the population. The government saw the Jews as an expendable minority, to be used as a safety valve for the dissatisfied
Polish masses. The problem arises, however, whether the
antisemitism so widespread in Poland can be explained
purely by economic factors. True, even the Catholic
church based its virulent antisemitism on supposedly economic grounds. Anti-Jewish boycotts were justified by the
church in the name of justice to the Polish laborer. "No
power will be able to stop the hatred" of Poles towards
Jews, but it had to be remembered, a Catholic paper said,
that "this hatred is highly beneficial to our Polish trade
and to our country."[9] On the other hand, antisemitic
Catholic priests in prewar Poland—there were very few
Catholic priests around then who were not antisemitic—
emphasized the corrupting influence of Jews on the morals
of the Polish population, and much was made of the traditional guilt of the Jews for rejecting the Messiah. It would
seem that a latent traditional antisemitism was exacerbated
by economic and social factors.

There were of course some Poles who stood up against
the antisemitic wave, especially among the liberals and the
Socialists, and among some of the peasant leaders. But the
cause of antisemitism was extremely popular in the thirties, and when in July 1938 the Polish government turned

to the Evian Conference on Refugees from Germany to discuss the fate of the Jewish refugees, and asked for havens for its Jews whom it wanted to get rid of, it knew that it was enjoying the support of the vast majority of the Polish populace.[10]

As Ringelblum described it, the attitude of the Poles to the Jews during the first year or so of the German occupation was not unequivocal. Polish middle-class people, most of the workers, and most of the intelligentsia felt varying degree of disgust towards the Nazi policy, which at that stage expressed itself in ghettoization, forced labor under degrading circumstances, expropriation of Jewish property, and expulsions from smaller towns, especially in the newly annexed western territories of the former Polish republic. There was some feeling of identification between the Poles, who were just one rung higher on the Nazi scale, and the Jews. But there is no doubt that ever-increasing numbers of Polish people benefited from the theft by the Nazis of Jewish property, though a large proportion of the loot remained in Nazi hands. Polish youths, radicalized even before the occupation of the country, and now under Nazi influence, turned against the defenseless Jews, who did not dare to react to physical attacks and acts of degradation.[11]

The deterioration in Polish-Jewish relations in the years 1940 to 1942 seen by both Ringelblum and more recent researchers can be explained on three different levels. On the political level, rumors were spreading that Jews had welcomed the Soviet conquerors of the ex-Polish eastern territories when the Soviet army entered these areas after 17 September 1939. The Polish people saw the Soviets as enemies, no less than the Germans. Any positive attitude toward the occupying forces was considered to be treason. And, indeed, there is much truth in the Polish claim that the Jews, in their vast majority, welcomed the Soviets. No wonder. The alternative, in those dark September days, was occupation by German forces, and the Russians were seen as saviors. Together with a section of the Belorussian and, to a much lesser extent, Ukrainian population, the Jews enthusiastically greeted the Soviet tanks rolling through the villages and townships of eastern Poland.[12]

Parts of the Jewish population maintained their positive attitude later on as well. Jewish students could study at Soviet institutes of higher learning free of charge and without a numerus clausus; poor artisans could coalesce into "artels" and earn their living, more or less in the accustomed manner; working-class people could reach positions in the administration and the police forces, could join the army and achieve officers' ranks, and so on. On the other hand, the majority of the Jewish population were engaged in petty trade, some were intellectuals, teachers, or rabbis, and there was a well-respected minority of middle-class merchants and industrialists. All these now suffered greatly; their businesses were confiscated, and they themselves were threatened with prolonged investigations and ultimate deportation. Jewish religious life was frowned upon and curtailed drastically; all the plethora of Jewish institutions, political parties, cultural clubs, schools, and newspapers were dissolved and abolished. A large part of Jewish public opinion swung against the Soviets as time went on, but of course could give no expression to such sentiments.

According to figures confidentially sent from the Polish embassy in the U.S.S.R. in 1941 and 1942, figures that seem to be reliable enough, the Soviets deported 880,000 ex-Polish citizens to labor and concentration camps in the Soviet Union, or 6.8 percent of the total population. Of these, 52 percent were Poles, 30 percent, or 264,000, were Jews, and 18 percent Ukrainians and Belorussians. There were 1.3 million Jews in these territories, so that the percentage of the deportees came to 20.1 percent, which was hardly a factor contributing to pro-Soviet enthusiasm.[13] Similar analyses and figures are available for the Baltic States and the territories annexed by the U.S.S.R. from Romania in 1940.[14]

It seems therefore clear that while the anti-Jewish wave among the Poles was based, politically, on a sentiment that had some basis in fact, this basis was purely transitory and was subjected to a very drastic change. However, while the factual basis for the antisemitic feeling may have changed, the feeling itself did not. Throughout the war the Polish underground allied to the Polish government-in-exile in London was to accuse the Jews of collaborating with the Soviet enemy. Paradoxically, this feeling was not shared in the Eastern territories, where the Jewish "treason" was supposed to have occurred. The only area where widespread Polish identification with the Jews took place was the East—Belorussia and Volhynia.

The second basis for anti-Jewish sentiment was the rapidly developing collusion of the Poles with the Nazi campaign of robbery and expropriation as applied to the Jews. The greater the benefit the Poles received from occupying Jewish apartments, taking over Jewish businesses and livelihoods, and taking away Jewish-owned furniture and clothing, the greater their interest in not seeing the Jews return to claim their erstwhile property. Many Jews were handing over their property for safekeeping with Polish acquaintances. In some cases these items were indeed held for the Jews who deposited them, and there were cases after the war where these properties were returned. But most of the Polish families appropriated these items, and when the Jews were deported, they acquired an interest in not seeing the former owners return to claim their property. Of the 25,000 or so testimonies of Holocaust survivors at Yad Vashem, a large proportion are from

Poland. Of these, many hundreds, if not more than that, testify to the accuracy of the generalization just made. As time went on, Poles could be heard to say that with all the disaster Hitler had brought to Poland, he had at least dealt with the Jewish question and solved it.[15]

The root cause for the overwhelmingly antisemitic sentiment among the Polish people at the time their Jewish neighbors were being murdered lay in the antisemitic preconditioning of the Polish nation, now coupled with very intensive Nazi propaganda. This propaganda, while not convincing wherever it applied itself to the persecuted and downtrodden Polish nation, was quite effective when turned against the Jews. Nor was the Catholic clergy any help at all. With some very honorable exceptions, the clergy by and large not only echoed the antisemitic sentiments, but led them. All this gained in effect by the Nazi policy of isolating the Jews completely from their environment. A comparison of Nazi policies against Jews in different European countries will show that extreme steps against the Jews were successful wherever the Nazis succeeded in breaking off all contact between their victims and the non-Jewish environment. This was certainly true of western and central Poland, where the ghettos were shut off from the Polish surroundings—whether hermetically as in the city of Lodz, or almost so in Warsaw or Lublin. Research now going on at the Institut für Zeitgeschichte in Munich, investigating the conversion of the Bavarian peasantry to Nazi antisemitism, has come to a similar conclusion: as long as the Jewish traders and peasants in the Bavarian countryside were part and parcel of a traditional scheme of social relationships, the peasants would not be persuaded by Nazi ideology. The change came after the Nazis had succeeded in isolating the Jews and had turned them into mysterious strangers living their lives at the edge of the village.

These three main factors were not, of course, static. As the war went on, and the Polish Communist party (the PPR) was reconstituted and started its military campaign against the German occupiers, anti-Communist Polish underground circles equated Jews with Communists and demanded an extermination campaign by their armed underground forces against both. Thus, Mieczyslaw Moczar, who later became the Minister of the Interior in the Polish Communist government in the sixties, wrote in June 1943 as follows: "Our detachments now have to fight on two fronts. The Command of the underground struggle is organizing detachments whose task it is to liquidate Communist bands, Soviet prisoners-of-war, and Jews."[16] General Bor-Komorowski, commander of the underground Home Army, who was later to lead the Polish Warsaw rebellion in August 1944, issued an order on 15 September 1943, explicitly commanding the extermination of Jewish partisan groups fighting in Polish forests, because he accused them of banditry.[17] Generally speaking, the attitude of the Home Army was antisemitic; no Jews known as such could join its ranks, and when the leaders of the Home Army were asked to help the Jewish Fighting Organization in Warsaw, the amount of help extended was ridiculously and tragically small: an organization that in 1941 claimed to possess 566 heavy machine guns, 1,097 light machine guns, 31,391 rifles, and five million units of ammunition, gave the Jews in Warsaw a total of seventy pistols, one hand machine gun, and one submachine gun. It claimed that it gave an additional five hundred hand grenades, but in fact it only gave some of the know-how—the actual grenades were homemade in the ghetto.[18] In Bialystok the Home Army refused to give anything at all.

The situation of the Jews trying to escape from the ghettos in the later stages of the war was desperate.

Groups of hooligans, so-called *szmalcowniki,* or black-mailers, were waiting for them to rob them of their money. Once they were penniless, they could not buy pro-tection, or food, from Polish citizens on the "Aryan" side of Polish cities. Defenseless and penniless, they were turned over by the *szmalcowniki* to the Nazi police.

Against this somber background of betrayal and inhu-manity, *schadenfreude* and murderous Jew-hatred, the small minority that risked their necks to help their Jewish neighbors stand out the sharper. It must be said right at the outset that it was much easier to be a friend of the Jews in Denmark or France, in Belgium or in Italy, than it was in Poland or in Lithuania, in the Ukraine or in Belorussia. Cases are known of Poles and their entire fami-lies executed for hiding Jews, their houses burnt, and their properties confiscated. It was very difficult to hide among the Polish population, partly because of the general an-tisemitic sentiment, and partly because of the imminent danger to the Poles who might have been willing to hide Jews. There were marked differences between the various areas of Poland in the number of Jews hiding among the Polish populace. While no accurate estimates have been reached as yet, it is clear from a comparison of testimonies that there is a marked congruence between the known in-cidence of antisemitism in a certain area and the unwill-ingness to aid Jews. Thus, few Jews managed to hide in the Kielce district, known for its strong, Catholic-oriented antisemitism. On the other hand in Volhynia, where the Poles were themselves a minority among the local Ukrain-ians, they were much more willing to help. Against the background of church antisemitism in an overwhelmingly Catholic country, the action of the Uniate archbishop of Lwow, Count Andreas Szeptycki, who ordered his clergy to save Jews despite his antisemitic views, stands out.[19] So do the actions of the Ursuline sisters, and other individual monastic houses and occasional village priests. It is difficult to estimate the number of Jews saved by hiding with local Polish people, but out of the about two million Polish Jews who were living in ethnic Polish areas, probably 1 percent or perhaps just slightly over that successfully hid. Ringelblum estimated the number of Jews hiding in Warsaw after the end of the Warsaw ghetto rebellion at twenty thousand but this appears to be very much exaggerated. Possibly ten thousand, or perhaps slightly more than that, hid.[20]

Organized action to save Jews was started in October 1942 by a Polish-Jewish group under Henryk Wolinski, called Zegota, set up by the official Polish underground, the political arm of the Home Army. Its activities were limited to Warsaw and, later, Cracow. It used about 1 percent of the funds transmitted by the Polish government in London to Poland.[21] The number of people saved by Żegota has been estimated at four thousand. In addition, Jewish self-help organizations, such as the Jewish Coordinating Council and its constituent bodies, the Bund and the Jewish National Council, accounted for some of the other people saved by hiding, especially again in Warsaw.

When we look at the total picture in the country of the largest Jewish population in Europe, we find that Jew-hatred did not decrease under the Nazis, but rather increased to a murderous degree. The majority of the population evinced an attitude of indifference which, in the circumstances, meant abandonment of the hunted Jews and noncooperation in their rescue. A minority of Poles were actively hostile. An even smaller minority were actively friendly. And yet, these people who tried to help, mostly working-class people, Socialists and Communists, liberal intellectuals and a smattering of clergy, aristocrats, and others, were individuals of truly heroic qualities, acting as they did in the most dangerous and difficult circumstances. Many of them paid with their lives for their heroism.

I have described the situation in Poland in some detail, because the position of the Jews in Polish society is so centrally important to our topic. The situation differed in different countries of Eastern Europe. Thus, a recent study of Jews in western Belorussia shows that comparatively large numbers of Jews in the areas of prewar northeastern Poland managed to escape into the jungle forests in that part of Europe and join or form partisan detachments fighting the Germans. Three factors are mentioned as determining this situation: the proximity of the forests, the sturdy quality of the Jewish villagers and inhabitants of the small townships in the area, and the relatively good relationships existing between the Belorussian peasants and their Jewish neighbors. Without being able to quote figures and percentages, one can say that if up to 10 percent of the Jewish population managed to escape despite the ferocity of the Nazi onslaught and the absence, in 1941 and 1942, of any widespread Soviet partisan movement, then that was at least partly due to the fact that the escaping Jew was less certain to be betrayed by a Belorussian than he was by a Lithuanian or a Ukrainian.[22]

In Lithuania and the western Ukraine on the other hand, the situation was worse than it was in ethnic Poland. In areas of Lithuania where no thick forests existed, the Jews were doomed, as they were in similar areas of the Ukraine. The ferocity of murderous Jew-hatred in those countries was, again, partly due to the real or supposed support of the Jews of the Soviet regime. Behind that there stood the age-old religious antagonism, coupled now with an extreme nationalist tendency. As in Poland, there were exceptions—less so in Lithuania, more so in the Ukraine. The diary, for instance, of the Lithuanian physician Dr. Helena Kutorgaine of Kaunas shows the kind of intrepid personality that was needed in that country to stand up not only to the Nazis but to the anti-Jewishness of the local population as well. In the Ukraine again, there were many individual cases of aid. Even a head of a township nominated by the Nazis could turn out to be a well-meaning person, such as engineer Lopatinski, for instance, of the East Galican township of Kosow, who at the risk of his own life saved a number of Jews in his own house and was encouraged to carry on by the local Orthodox priest. Similarly, the small Baptist minority in the Ukraine, some few thousand souls perhaps, scattered in small villages and homesteads, loom very large indeed in the stories of survivors. Themselves persecuted as a religious minority, they saw the Jews as the Agnus Dei, to be helped and succored whatever the risk and whatever the cost.

In the forests of Belorussia and the northern Ukraine, where most of the Soviet partisan detachments were established in late 1942, in 1943, and in 1944, the relations of Gentiles to Jews were not simple either. They were supposedly fighting on the same side, but antisemitism was rampant in many of these units, up to and including the murder of Jewish comrades-in-arms. One can mention, for instance, the case of the Voroshilov partisan detachment under the command of the Fyodor Markov, who took away arms from a Jewish detachment of the Jewish resistance movement in Vilna under Joseph Glasman that had joined his group and thus practically sentenced them to death. There seems little doubt but that this action stemmed from an anti-Jewish attitude.[23] There were many such cases, along with others where such antisemitic tendencies were scotched by the energetic intervention of partisan commanders. The general impression is that Jews had better chances under Russian commanders, and their chances were worst under Ukrainian commanders, though again a generalization would have to take into account exceptions.

The situation in the Balkan area and East Central Europe is too complicated to lend itself to a brief analysis. Yet a few salient points might be mentioned. In Slovakia, for instance, where there was a fairly large population of some 90,000 Jews in 1940,[24] the expulsion of over 58,000 Jews to Poland caused a change of mood among large sections of the Slovak population. Soon after the deportations, rumors began to circulate that these Jews had been sent to their deaths. Opposition was especially marked among the minority churches—Protestants of various colorings—and the Czech minority. The Hungarian minority's representative in the Slovak parliament was the only one who voted against the anti-Jewish measures. In the more remote villages antigovernment feelings began to show themselves in spontaneous steps taken to protect individual Jews.[25] The main reason for this change in atmosphere was not connected with the Jews, but with the unpopularity of the war against Russia, in which Slovak troops had to participate, and with the losses in lives that this entailed. There seems to be little doubt, however, that the revulsion against the deportation of the Jews was a contributory factor. Only the Catholic clergy and parts of the nationalistically-inclined middle class and intelligentsia continued to support the anti-Jewish line almost to the end. The participation of Jews in the so-called Slovak National Uprising in August 1944 was very marked. Many Jews joined the ranks of the Communists, who appeared to be the most extreme anti-Nazi force in the country.

It would seem that in Slovakia a very strongly antisemitic tradition broke down at least in part, because of the overall growth of an anti-German national feeling on the one hand, and moral revulsion on the other hand, especially among minority groups and opponents of the regime. A similar trend seems to have occurred in Bulgaria, where the realization that Germany was losing the war combined in the spring of 1943 with pressure from the opposition to the government and perhaps an element of moral revulsion on the part of the Orthodox Church. In any case, the Bulgarian developments were no less surprising in a sense than those in Slovakia, because there sections of the Fascist clique ruling the country initiated the protest against the decision to deport the Jews to their deaths. The king either joined this protest or possibly even prodded it in the first place. Such divergent forces as the Orthodox establishment and the Communists made their opposition to the planned expulsion known. All this took place in a country where economic and religious antisemitism was rampant, and where the population up to that point seemed to have had no qualms about brutally and cynically robbing their Jewish neighbors, with whom they had been living for many centuries, of all their possessions. Unfortunately, Bulgarian archives are not open to inspection, and as long as free research in that country remains impossible, there will be many more questions than answers.[26]

Romania is another great puzzle, and as yet not a single study exists on the fate of the Jews in that country during the Holocaust, not to speak of the problem of Romanian-Jewish relations. Much more than Bulgaria, Romania was a hotbed of the most virulent forms of antisemitism in the nineteenth and early twentieth centuries. This was motivated by the now already familiar mixture of religious, economic, and cultural elements, exacerbated by the chauvinistic nationalism of interwar Romania. The loss of Bessarabia and northern Bukovina to the U.S.S.R. in June 1940 was blamed on the Jews. The Fascist regime set up by the Iron Guard and Marshall Ion Antonescu in the summer of that year explicitly sought the wholesale economic despoliation and ultimate expulsion of all Jews, who now numbered between 300,000 and 350,000 in the truncated kingdom.[27] A terrible pogrom at Iasi and savage slaughter at Bucharest followed. Even the internal revolution in early 1941 which removed the Iron Guard from power and established a military dictatorship under Antonescu did not change the situation—the declared aim of the government remained the same. Expropriation of property, removal from occupations, and slave labor by Jewish men followed. And yet, when in the spring of 1942 the Nazis demanded that Romania follow the example given by the Slovak government, which had agreed to the deportation of Slovak Jews to Poland and had even paid the Nazis for every Jew thus transported to the gas chambers, the Romanians vacillated, and in the end refused the German request. Though we are still waiting for a detailed study to analyze these events, it appears that uncertainty about the outcome of the war and the desire not to burn all bridges to the Western powers, as well as anti-German sentiments among nationalist Romanians who were accusing German military commanders of sacrificing Romanian divisions on the Russian front in order to save German lives, all played a part. Brutal pogroms accompanying robbery of Jewish property—yes, that could fit in with local chauvinistic and antisemitic traditions; but total mass murder, of which the Romanian government was well informed, was a different matter.[28]

There is very little evidence of a humane attitude on the part of the Romanian population. The rescue of the Romanian Jews from total destruction is attributable less to popular sentiment or moral considerations than to very practical military and political factors that decided the policy of the Antonescu government. Interestingly, the antisemitic canard about the all-powerful World Jewry which was supposedly in control of the capitalist powers was a positive element in the situation: the Romanian government thought that it might be worthwhile to try to use Romanian Jewry as a pawn in future contacts with the West, where the all-powerful Jews would press the democratic governments into a peace arrangement in order to safeguard the lives of their fellow Jews. This was not the only country where antisemitism had that paradoxical effect.

The breaking up of Yugoslavia by the Nazis created another complicated situation. Of the 75,000 Yugoslav Jews, 14,000 remained in Serbia where Nazi rule was very thinly veiled by an ineffective puppet government. They were quickly murdered by Nazi troops, with only a few escaping into the mountains. Thirty-four thousand others found themselves in Croatia, a Fascist puppet state that permitted itself excesses against the Jews of a brutality that surpassed almost anything known in Nazi Europe. However, over a third of Croat Jewry managed to flee into the areas of the country occupied by Italian troops. There, under the benevolent General Roatta, Jewish lives were safe. Croat murderousness expressed itself against Serbs to almost the same extent as it did towards Jews; as a result, Jews tended to experience widely disparate treatment at the hands of the local population. In Serbia, the local populace was friendly and helpful, as were the Italians in the coastal areas. Important elements among the Croat population supported, at first at least, the Fascist government of Ante Pavelic. No succor could be expected for the Jews from the local urban populations of Zagreb or Osijek. On the other hand, as time went on and the Nazi occupation proved more and more onerous, the Croat-led Tito partisan movement gained ground, and its bitter enmity towards the Nazis included a defense of Jewish lives wherever possible. The tiny Jewish minority in Yugoslavia played a disproportionately large part in the resistance movement. As parts of the Croat population veered towards an anti-Nazi stand, the Serbian royalists under Draja Mihajlović tended more and more to withdraw from active combat against the Germans, and their attitude towards Jews became neutral to hostile. The churches, Orthodox in Serbia and Catholic in Croatia, played an insignificant role in determining the attitude of Serbs and Croats towards the Jews. It seems that in Croatia a bitter antagonism to the Jews changed partly as a result of extraneous developments. As larger sections of the population identified with the partisan movement, so the impact of antisemitism lessened.[29]

A completely different situation again existed in Italy. There the population, the church, and the Fascist government were either indifferent or actively friendly towards the small Jewish minority of some 40,000 souls and the Jewish refugees in Italian-occupied southeastern France and Yugoslavia. Antisemitism was more the result of a conscious aping of Nazi attitudes among a very small section of the Italian Fascist party. Apart from these few active and influential officials, Italian Jews hardly encountered animosity. There was no attempt in Italy to isolate the Jews, and when Jews were persecuted, shipped off to Auschwitz or interned in local camps, this was always at the behest of the Germans or their direct and extreme supporters. After the summer of 1943, when the south of the country had fallen to the Allies and an Italian Fascist Republic was established in the north under the direct rule of the Nazis, the attitude of the population at large to the Jews was one of commiseration and, very often, of active help. Cardinal Pietro Boetto of Genoa and Don Francesco Repetto, his secretary, established a network of aid to Jews, and various monastic houses helped as well. Liberals, Socialists, and Communists in Italian partisan units in the north included many Jews who saw themselves as Italians first, and who out of an Italian patriotism helped Jewish victims of the hated Nazi conquerors.[30]

There is a striking similarity between the situations in Italy, Denmark, and the Low Countries. Denmark, as is well known, rescued most of its about 8,000 Jews to neighboring Sweden (actually, there were 7,220 Danish Jewish refugees in Sweden at the end of the war; 475 were caught and deported by the Nazis). The reasons, as Leni Yahil has pointed out, are largely connected with the way the Danish people regarded themselves, their traditions, and their aspirations. The Danes saw their democratic traditions endangered by the German occupation. A threat to the Jews meant an attack on their self-understanding as a free people, because the Jews were either Danish citizens or protected refugees. The attack on Danish democracy was interpreted as an attack on the basis of Danish public morality. Danish nationalism was understood as identical with a democratic, freedom-loving way of life. The Jews were therefore protected not because they were particularly liked; the question of the Jews as such simply did not enter into the picture at all. The Danes saw themselves confronted by a threat to their own national identity. It so happened that the occasion for that was the Jewish problem, which arose in October 1943 in the form of the Nazi desire to deport the Jews. The half-spontaneous action of the Danish resistance movement, widely supported by the local population, was the starting point for active resistance to the German occupation.

In the rescue of Danish Jewry the Protestant clergy played a prominent part. Individuals like Frederik Torm or Johannes Nordentoft explained the godlessness of Nazi antisemitic doctrine, and they were listened to. Their preaching and writing belonged to that same consensus of

Danish self-understanding that led to the rescue action.[31]
In Denmark, just as in Italy, a combination of anti-Nazi
sentiments and democratic nationalism reinforced humanitarian considerations derived from religious convictions.
The Jews were not regarded as good or bad, but as people
in danger who had to be helped for one's own communal
or personal moral well-being.

We find something very similar to that combination in
Belgium. There, out of a Jewish population of about
57,000 in 1940–41, 29,000 survived. Belgian Jews
organized to help themselves—in contrast to Danish Jews,
who remained totally passive—and were aided by the
Belgian underground, and the major dignitaries of the
Catholic church in the country, such as Cardinal Van Roey
of Antwerp or Bishop Kerkhofs of Liège. Thousands of
Jewish children were hidden by such organizations as the
Oeuvre National d'Enfance under Mlle. Yvonne Nevejean
and by Communist and Socialist bodies. King Leopold of
Belgium and especially his mother, Queen Elizabeth, were
active in saving Jewish people by interventions and direct
aid. The Belgian government-in-exile in London was the
only such body to declare unequivocally that it would not
recognize any act of repression or expropriation of Jews,
thus undercutting Nazi attempts to create a community of
interests between the murderers and those who benefited
materially from the murder.

There was, however, a marked distinction in attitudes
to Jews between the two ethnic communities that made up
the Belgian kingdom: the Flemings and the Walloons.
Antisemitism was, for reasons that have not been properly
investigated, stronger in the Flemish areas than in the
Walloon districts. This is true for the prewar period as
well as for the war years. During the war, the Nazis pro-
jected the idea of a new order in Europe based on the pre-
dominance of the Germanic peoples, of whom the Flem-

ings were a part. This same idea was propagated in Holland as well, and failed to make more than a very partial dent in the anti-German stance of the Dutch. In Flanders it had much more of an effect. The attitude towards the Jews was therefore much less friendly there than in the Walloon section; but that is relative, because among the Flemish people, too, there were many, including much of the religious and intellectual leadership, who actively opposed Nazi anti-Jewish policies. In the Walloon areas, opposition to Nazi antisemitism can be described as popular and widespread, despite the fact that prior to the war Belgian attitudes to Jews were not marked by any clear rejection of antisemitism. It appears that the hatred of the German occupant, coupled with a democratic background and a humanitarian interpretation of religious and secular political dogmas, made the difference.[32]

We find a similar attitude in Holland. In February 1941 the Dutch workers, led by their Socialist and Communist leadership, declared a general strike in support of the Jews or, perhaps, in protest against anti-Jewish actions of the German occupying authorities. The strike was broken by the Jews themselves, whose leadership, cowed and frightened and threatened with reprisals unless the strike ended, appealed to the workers to call it off. The Nazis then succeeded in imposing this leadership on the Jewish community, and largely succeeded also in isolating the Jews from their Dutch neighbors. As in Denmark and in the French parts of Belgium, however, it seems that the fight for Jewish lives became a main expression in a purely Dutch resistance struggle against the hated Nazi jackboot. In Holland, as in Belgium but unlike in Denmark, the Jewish population actively sought ways out of the impasse, despite the spinelessness of their leaders. It is estimated that about 24,000 out of the 140,000 Jews in Holland hid with Dutch people. Only 16,000 of these survived; the others were caught by the Nazis, in most cases because of the betrayal by pro-Nazi Dutch elements.

While Dutch identification with the Jews has been exaggerated and the part played by Nazi sympathizers underrated, it is nevertheless true that the Dutch population, especially the intellectual, political, and religious leadership, by and large opposed the Nazi policies, including those against the Jews, with determination.[33]

Unlike the Belgians and the Dutch, many people in France favored collaboration with the German occupants. The government of the old *Maréchal* Philippe Pétain in Vichy enjoyed the support of large sections of the peasantry, the middle classes, the army, and the old aristocracy. Antisemitism had been as strong, if not stronger, in France as in Germany or Russia. With the defeat of France in June 1940 and the general xenophobia that spread in the country as a result of blaming the French collapse on foreign influences, antisemitic tendencies became very strong indeed. The northern half of France was under direct German occupation, and anti-Jewish measures naturally started there. Escalating in 1941 and early 1942, they spread into the unoccupied section of the country, and seemed to command reasonably general approval by the supporters of the regime. France is, of course, a predominantly Catholic country, and Pétain wanted to be sure that his anti-Jewish actions would not be condemned by the Vatican. In the summer of 1941, French ambassador Léon Bérard at the Vatican assured his chief of state that "an authorized person at the Vatican" had told him that "they have no intention of quarreling with us over the Jewish statute." The Vatican expected the Vichy authorities not to forbid intermarriage of Christians with Jews, and hoped that principles of justice and charity would be observed in the liquidation of Jewish businesses.[34]

This is not to say that there was not another France in

existence at the same time—a republican, anti-Nazi, socialist, liberal France dedicated to secularist or Christian humanism. But it seems that it was in a minority. There were groups and individuals who tried to protect Jews or at least help them. Among them one may count the Abbé Glasberg, a Jewish convert to Christianity and a close collaborator of the French Cardinal Gerlier of Lyon, the Primat des Gaulles. Others included the Protestant leader Marc Boegner, head of CIMADE, a Protestant social agency. The Communists had their own aid organizations and they were effective in protecting their Jewish members from the worst effects of the anti-Jewish decrees. A roof organization of over twenty social agencies was founded at Nîmes in November 1940 to help Jews interned in French concentration camps in the unoccupied zone.[35]

The breaking point came with the beginning of the mass deportations of Jews from France to Poland, in July 1942 in the north and in August in the south. The deportations were carried out in a most brutal and horrible way. They included the separation of four thousand Jewish children from their parents and their transport in sealed trains to Auschwitz where they were of course immediately murdered. The brutal deportations seem to have caused a revulsion of feeling against the Nazi policies. Not that this included all sections of the French population. However, when Jewish organizations acted resolutely to save as many people, especially children, as possible, they received help from a large number of French individuals and institutions. Jewish groups trying to save children were especially active. The OSE (Oeuvre de Secours aux Enfants) organized a widespread network of hiding places for Jewish children, mostly with individual peasant families or with religious institutions. Other Jewish groups followed suit, and as a result about seven thousand children were hidden in France. As far as I know, there is not a single recorded case of betrayal to the authorities of any of these children. Most of them were hidden in the south of France. There, the pastoral letter of Archbishop Saliege of Toulouse enjoining upon his flock to aid the Jews (22 August 1942) had great influence. Similarly, Bishop Theas of Montauban, and some of the collaborators of Abbé Glasberg, such as the Jesuit Fr. Chaillet, were very effective in placing children with families and institutions.[36]

The impression that there were two parallel French entities, one supporting the Vichy regime and one opposing it, or one willing to accept German dictates and the other fighting them, which one gets from the vast literature that has appeared on France during the war years, is confirmed when one studies the Jewish problem. One part of the French people was extending a helping hand to the Jews, while another was busy helping the Nazis to round them up and deport them to their deaths. Archbishop Suhart of Paris voiced no objection at all to Nazi measures against the Jews; on the contrary, he maintained correct and even friendly relations with Nazis. Most, but not all, prefects in provincial towns collaborated with the Vichy regime, including its special anti-Jewish militia. And yet, the fact that seven thousand children could be hidden without betrayal seems to argue for the view that there must have been a fairly widespread mood in favor of helping people in distress who happened to be Jews.

This impression is fortified by a piece of research done by a student of mine some years ago in a typical French village which had hidden Jewish children. The peasants there had been brought up in a typical antisemitic tradition based on Christian anti-Jewish prejudices. They supported the old *Maréchal* and his national government in Vichy. They had had no real immediate contact with actual Jews until the organizer of OSE appeared on the scene and placed children with the peasants, asking to hide them not only from Germans but from the legitimate militia forces of a government of which they generally approved. It appears that the antisemitic stereotype which they had lived with either broke down or was ignored or superseded, because there as elsewhere, they accepted the children, hid them, and refused to betray them. It also appears that this experience did not really alter their stereotyped image of the Jews in general, though that would have to be confirmed by more satisfactory research.[37] The question is, under what conditions do antisemitic stereotypes become determinants of social and political action, and where do they recede before other considerations, such as considerations of ordinary human decency? It is of course impossible to draw any conclusions from a single, random example and the whole problem is wide open to further investigation.

When we consider not differences between countries and nationalities, but the behavior of political and religious institutions, we encounter similarly perplexing varieties of response. It should have become clear by now that there can be no talk of the behavior of *the* Catholic church, though one can legitimately talk of the Vatican's policy. That policy was one of extreme caution, lack of commitment, and a desire not to endanger relationships with Nazi Germany and its millions of Catholics, who were fighting a war against the Bolshevik atheist menace. The Vatican did intervene diplomatically in certain places, such as Slovakia and Hungary, but its interventions were always circumspect and secret. It encouraged the saving of Jewish lives by prelates who cared to ask for its advice. It offered some, but by no means sufficient, facilities to the Jews of Rome itself—had the Vatican declared that it would not allow the deportation of Roman Jews and had it opened its many Roman institutions to the endangered Jews, it is clear to us as it was clear then that the Jews of

Rome would have been saved. In that sense the Vatican bears a heavy responsibility.[38]

Yet, when one considers the response of church dignitaries, priests, or just ordinary believers, one finds the most amazing variety of responses. In Germany itself the famous sermons of Cardinal Michael Faulhaber in late 1933 praised pre-Christian Judaism, though one would be very hard put to point to any concrete actions of Catholic German dignitaries in favor of Jews. Cardinal Szeptycki in Lwow was an important, but rare, exception to the general attitude of the Polish priesthood. The princes of the church ranged from Saliege in Toulouse to the Papal Nuncio at Bratislava who, when asked by Rabbi Weissmandel whether the church should not intervene to save at least the innocent blood of Jewish children, answered, "Es gibt kein unschuldiges jüdisches Kinderblut, jedes jüdische Blut ist schuldig." ("There is no innocent Jewish children's blood, all Jewish blood is guilty.")[39] The priests ranged from martyrs to murderers, just as all the rest of the people did. The same applies to the Protestants—the Danish professors of theology who attacked antisemitism, Probst Heinrich Grüber in Berlin who organized help for the persecuted German Jews, and Marc Boegner of France were at one end of the scale; the Deutsche Christen who collaborated fully with the Nazis were at the other end. For the Communists, there was no Jewish problem at all—it would all be solved in the coming revolutionary upheaval. But in the meantime, all energies had to be directed against the Nazis, and as the Jews were being persecuted by the Nazi regime, they were natural allies. Polish Communists were the only ones who would accept Jews into their fighting groups; during the Warsaw ghetto rebellion, attempts were made by the ill-equipped and small Communist detachments of the Gwardia Ludowa to mount attacks on the Nazis besieging the ghetto. In the forests, convinced Communists often fought against overt antisemitism in their units. Belgian and French Communists helped to hide Jews from the eyes of the Nazis. On the other hand, Soviet Communists dissolved Jewish units, declared that the defense of Jewish noncombatants in the forests was none of their business; German Communists demanded of their Jewish comrades to establish their own underground groups (the groups of Herbert Baum and Heinz Joachim, which were caught and liquidated by the Gestapo in 1942). Yet on the whole, left-wing political groups were, with some exceptions, inclined to help Jewish victims of Nazism. Among the others, no patterns can be discerned. Family background, personal convictions, and in the end what one may call moral fiber decided the attitude of the Gentile to the Jew.

Germany itself poses perhaps the most difficult problem of all. How much did the ordinary German know of what was done in his name to Jews in Europe? What was his attitude? Was Nazi antisemitism an ideology superimposed on the Germans by the Hitler dictatorship, was the murder campaign a deed done by a small minority in the name of a majority who were not asked for their opinions? Or was there a general consensus on the Jewish question among most Germans, a consensus that allowed the murder to be committed without any significant resistance on the part of the civilized German people?

It is a fact that there was very little resistance, though there were cases of Germans who risked their lives to defend Jewish people. It is a fact that rumors were both spread and believed that Jews were somehow done away with somewhere in the East. It is equally a fact that Himmler complained, in his famous speech to SS officers in Poznan on 4 October 1943, that "they all come trudging, eighty million worthy Germans, and each one has his one decent Jew. Sure, the others are swine, but this one is an A-1 Jew."[40] If Himmler is to be believed, then, Nazi racial ideology did not completely succeed in penetrating the German mind. It is also a fact that after the war, over 1,100 Jews emerged from their hiding places in Berlin, where they had been protected by their German neighbors, mostly in the working-class sections of the city.[41]

It is only recently that a large number of the so-called *Lageberichte* of the SD have become available.[42] These are reports by the security police of the SS on the mood of the German population before and during the war. While it is definitely premature to summarize these reports, much less to evaluate them, it would seem at first blush that the attitude of the German population was characterized more by apathy, indifference, discomfort at the thought of what was happening to the Jews, and fear of the Nazi authorities, than by active agreement with Nazi policies, whose general content was either known or correctly guessed.

It is clear, I think, from this cursory *tour d'horizon,* that any generalizations regarding the attitude of Gentiles to Jews during the Holocaust must be approached with the greatest diffidence. Of the generalizations that will hold water, one might mention these: in Poland, Lithuania, Latvia, and the Ukraine, in Croatia and Romania, the attitude of the overwhelming majority of the local population, including that of the majority churches, and excepting the left-wing political parties, ranged from hostile indifference to active hostility. Countries that saved most of their Jews were Bulgaria, Denmark, Belgium, and France. There is little in common between the democratic character of Protestant Denmark and the unfortunate traditions of Orthodox Bulgaria, yet the fate of the Jewish communities was similar, though the reasons for the rescue were not. There were vast differences between Walloon Belgium and a split French society, yet the percentages of Jews saved were similar. Minority churches tended to protect Jewish minorities. Growing opposition to Germany usually meant greater readiness to help the Jewish neighbor. Religious convictions had apparently less to do with attitudes to Jews than did national backgrounds, historical traditions, or political views. On the whole, the tragic situation of the Jew in a Gentile environment was one in which the Jew could only appeal to feelings of mercy, compassion, and loving kindness. In some places he met people who had these qualities; in most places he did not. He had no power at all to appeal to other sentiments or practical considerations, except perhaps when these stemmed from mistaken antisemitic hallucinations. The Jew was powerless, and the European background of antisemitism did not permit for more than a very partial reassertion of humanism in the attitude toward him.

The problem of the attitude of the Allied nations, mainly of course of the United States and Great Britain, to the European Jews caught up in the Holocaust has been partly dealt with in recent literature. Arthur Morse has set the tone in his volume *While Six Million Died* with a general accusation of complicity in the murder by inaction, based on ill-will and stupidity.[43] Interestingly enough, Morse's accusation is directed against the United States government, not the people of the United States, and is based on the idea that Americans had all the necessary information at their disposal to act to save Jews even before the news regarding the murder itself was received in August 1942. A more differentiated analysis does not produce quite the same impression. It is of course perfectly true that pathological antisemites such as Breckinridge Long in the State Department exercised control over such vital areas as visas of entry to the United States. What Morse and some of the others tend to ignore is the fact that the antisemitic stand was supported by a very large section of American public opinion.[44] Published studies indicate that close to one half of the American people were expressing differing shades of antisemitism right up to 1942 and 1943. In addition, there was throughout the thirties a very strong restrictionist sentiment militating against large immigration into the United States. The constant fear of knowledgeable liberals was that if bills were introduced into Congress to change the immigration quotas, the quotas would indeed be changed, but not upwards. In such a case there was a real possibility of drastic quota restrictions or even an abolition, temporarily perhaps, of quotas altogether.

Feingold and Friedman have pointed out that Roosevelt was performing a balancing act between liberal and isolationist opinion, on the refugee question no less than on others. The problem was, as they have argued, that an avowedly liberal administration did not take the bull by the horns, did not try to change the climate of opinion by imaginative leadership; more importantly even, the administration did not utilize these tools that were legitimately its own in trying to help Jews and, possibly, other people persecuted by the Nazis up to America's entry into the war. The conference convened by the United States at Evian in July 1938 was a political ploy to appease liberal opinion at home rather than an earnest attempt to aid the victims of Nazi persecutions by finding new homes for them. The United States was not ready to offer such homes, and the other states were not more accommodating.[45] After a year of increased immigration into the United States within the limits of the quota system, in 1938–39, the State Department's restrictionists prevented the filling of the meager quotas and thus condemned legitimate candidates for immigration to suffering and persecution.

There is no doubt that the restrictionists in the State

Department reflected the antisemitic tendencies of some sectors of the American public generally. In other words, the failure to aid the Jews under Hitler's rule was in part a reflection of an antisemitic trend. As for the other factors, the main one seems to have been the feeling that the Jewish question was not that central or important. The administration consistently tried to cover up the fact that the Hitler regime was persecuting Jews, and not Germans who held all kinds of different beliefs. This attitude was in line with that of the major Jewish bodies in America who wished to keep a very low profile in the face of the anti-Jewish mood, and mostly insisted that they had little in common with German or Central European Jews apart from their religion. The paradox is that Hitler was persecuting the Jews as a race, as a people, while Americans, including the major non-Zionist bodies in American Jewry, were dealing with individuals supposedly persecuted for their religious and political beliefs. The administration did not wish to see what should have been perfectly obvious from the simple reading of Nazi newspapers: the Jewish victims were just that, namely Jews, and not nondescript German persecutees.

There was no need to know of the mass murder in order to save as many European Jews as possible by bringing them into the New World. What was published in the American press was quite sufficient: the persecutions and degradations of German Jews until 1938; the pogroms of November 1938; the mass arrests of Jews and their murderous treatment in the Nazi concentration camps in 1938 and 1939; the establishment of the ghettos, and the attendant waves of hunger, epidemics, and death. All this was presented in the press, photographed by newsmen who until 1941 could still visit Eastern Europe. The suffering of hundreds of thousands, soon of millions, was evident enough for consciences to be aroused, for steps to be taken. Nothing was done.

Morse argues in his book that the West received information about the mass murders of European Jewry from Geneva in August 1942. He is wrong on two counts: the August message from Geneva was hesitant, uncertain, and obscure; it did not say that Jews were being systematically murdered, but only that such a plan was reportedly going to be put into operation later on in 1942. In the second place, however, the West was not dependent on the Geneva cable. As early as June 1942 detailed descriptions of the Nazi murder plan and its execution in practice had been transmitted to the West and published widely.[46] The problem lies elsewhere: the thing was unbelievable, and indeed was not believed. Can you really blame the Anglo-American statesmen for not believing this unbelievable story? Did the Jews in the West believe it? More than that—did the Jews who were living through it believe it? Do those who survived it believe their own memories and nightmares? In the end this boils down to an epistemological question: when does information become internalized knowledge, and when does this knowledge become a guide to action? The information regarding the Holocaust was there in the late spring of 1942, about one whole year after the Nazis had begun the mass murder of European Jewry with their invasion of the U.S.S.R. (June 1941). The point was that it took time before it became knowledge. As far as the Western powers were concerned, it became a guide to action partly, very late, or not at all.

One may assume that some members of the administration began to believe in the correctness of the information at the end of 1942. On 17 December 1942, at the instigation of the Polish government-in-exile and the British government, the Allied nations issued a proclamation against the murder of the Jews—the only one of its kind throughout the war. It was followed by exemplary inaction. The Anglo-American conference on refugees at Bermuda, in April 1943, decided that as long as the war was on, nothing could be done for the Jews persecuted by the Nazis. Some help might possibly be extended to those few who managed to cross into neutral territory, mainly Spain. No negotiations regarding Jews or other refugees could be permitted with the enemy; no ransom could be paid. We know today, and it was stated by Jewish bodies at the time, that only some kind of negotiation might have saved lives. We know, and it was argued in 1944, that only certain types of military action, such as the bombing of death camps, the bombing of railway lines leading to the camps, or the mass dropping of parachutists to encourage armed resistance, might have been effective. We know, and it was argued then, that certain types of intervention with neutrals and with the International Red Cross might have caused the Nazis to allow the sending of parcels and the exit of children. We know now, and the State Department and the Foreign Office in Britain knew then, that the Nazis were eager to exchange German ethnics from the free world for Jewish children. Even after the information regarding the murder was believed, very little was done.

Why? There is no logical, political explanation. From a purely military point of view, from an internal political point of view, there was no reason not to help. As 1943 progressed, the influence of the antisemitic crowd in the State Department lessened. At the end of the year, a small group of dedicated democrats and liberals, non-Jews, who worked for the Treasury Department, moved their Jewish secretary, Henry Morgenthau, Jr., to pound the table and demand action to save the remnants of European Jewry. The public mood had changed, and Roosevelt, ever sensitive to such changes, declared the establishment of a War

Refugee Board, on 22 January 1944, to try to rescue Jews and other immediately threatened people. For the next fifteen months, the WRB, directed for most of that period by John W. Pehle, did a great deal to rescue Jews and others. The WRB was a unique case of humanitarian and moral considerations superseding political and utilitarian arguments in the midst of a terrible war. But even the WRB could not bring itself to support military activities such as the bombardment of Auschwitz and the railways leading up to it. It transferred funds into Nazi Europe that helped people to survive, but it did not ask the government or the American public for help. Even now the Jews were left to fend for themselves. Every penny transferred to Europe was Jewish money. Contrary to legend, the Jews were still a basically powerless community, even though now some of the people in control were willing and eager to help.

The same description applies basically to the British attitude to Jews under Nazi rule, except that in Britain public opinion was much more alert to the desperate position of European Jewry. One does not hear a great deal of American church dignitaries in connection with protests against what was being done to the Jews. In Britain, the Archbishop of Canterbury and the Roman Catholic Archbishop of Westminster were prime movers in every step taken to prod the government into some sort of action. In America, the administration followed the lead of public opinion. In Britain, it lagged behind it. With some difficulty, and with a steadfastness worthy of a better cause, the British Foreign and Colonial offices as well as the traditionally anti-Jewish military establishment stood up against the pressure of MPs, newspapers, and the clergy, who demended that something be done to save the Jews while the war was still on. To the argument that the only solution to the problem of Jewish suffering at the hand of the Nazis was to win the war quickly, the retort was made that if something was not done in the meantime, there would be no one left to welcome victory. The impression one gains from intensive reading of British official files of the Foreign Office is that British officialdom was not reflecting the mood of the British people, who, in many letters and touching appeals, expressed a view that stood in crass contradiction to the line taken at the Bermuda conference and thereafter.

After the establishment of the WRB in January 1944 British policy towards the Jews differed greatly from that of the United States. The British government took exception to the steps taken by the WRB to smuggle money into Nazi Europe, to help Jews who were hiding in France, in Slovakia, or in Germany; they were even more unhappy about the negotiations that were started between the Jews represented by Saly Mayer, JDC representative in Switzerland, and the SS in August 1944. The fact that the American government, grudgingly and half-heartedly, supported these talks was not accepted by the British.

There is no need to waste any energy in describing the Soviet attitude—there simply was none. There was no positive Soviet step to defend Jews or to rescue them. The Soviet Union was fighting the Nazi invader, who was murdering Jews, amongst other things. Obviously, anything the U.S.S.R. did to defeat the Nazis was favorable to the survival of Jews. Jews fled into the Soviet interior, or tried to, when the Nazis came. At first, Soviet guards were stationed along the pre-1939 Soviet borders and prevented Jews from the Baltic countries and eastern Poland to flee into the Soviet heartland. Later these guards were taken away, and hundreds of thousands escaped. Nobody cared for them; perhaps nobody could have, in the chaos and disorientation of the first Soviet defeats. Masses of Jews survived despite hunger and typhoid. Masses died of hunger and typhoid and in the Soviet concentration camps

where large numbers of Jews had been put between late
1939 and June 1941. Appeals to Russia to take specific action to protect Jews fell on deaf ears. Appeals to bomb
Auschwitz in 1944 were not even answered. All contact
with the Nazis designed to rescue people or keep them
alive until the end of the war was disallowed. There was, I
think, no active antisemitism involved in the Russian official attitude, just a general lack of concern with human
lives and human values.

Even a cursory glance at the attitude of the major Allies
to the Jews under Nazi rule makes clear that we are dealing with a complicated phenomenon. In America there
were people of the ilk of Breckinridge Long, but there
were people like John W. Pehle as well. In Britain, the
Prime Minister himself intervened a couple of times to
impress upon his officials the need to do something, but
even a Prime Minister could not break through the barrier
of officialdom. The motivations for the largely unhelpful
attitude of both powers differed in details, but there appear to me to exist some common elements. Antisemitism
was a more important factor in the United States than it
was in Britain. Nor can the British attitude be properly
termed apathetic. The term apathy would fit the American
attitude much better. Official Britain was concerned with
the possibility that Jews might be unloaded onto her in
large numbers, about the possibility of Nazi infiltration
into Jewish refugee transports, and about the danger that
any action concerned with alleviating the lot of Jews
might prolong the war. The refugee question generally,
and the Jewish problem specifically, was a bothersome
minor point that was endangering Anglo-American cooperation on the major issue, which was the defeat of Nazi
Germany. When the Holocaust became known in the
West in 1943 and 1944, this became just another reason
to defeat the Nazis quickly. Except for the British fear of

Jewish refugees flooding the West if they were released by the Nazis as a result of negotiations, the United States shared these British apprehensions. But the most basic common denominator was quite simply that the Jewish problem, the murder of a whole people, just did not appear important enough to cause the Western Allies to take drastic steps to remedy the situation. The fact of the matter was that the Jews, to misquote Stalin in another context, did not have any political battalions that counted. The Western Allies were fighting the war for decency, for liberty, and against the most terrible totalitarian regime that had ever disgraced the face of the earth. They were fighting a war in defense of certain moral values that had been challenged. In that war, sight was lost of the purpose for which it was fought, when no steps were taken to prevent the continuation of the Holocaust.

Finally, let me make some comments on the attitudes of the neutrals. As mentioned above, the present stage of research enables one to deal with only two of these countries, and even there one has to tread very carefully indeed. Much that has been written and said about Spain seems to be based on a misreading of the evidence. Spain had very little interest in the humanitarian aspect of the refugee question. Until El Alamein and Stalingrad, Franco hoped for an Axis victory. His country, however, was a mass of ruins as a result of the civil war, and the West held some very important economic trump cards vis-à-vis Spain. Until late 1942 Jews could cross through Spanish territory if they had visas to Portugal. Illegal crossings through the Pyrenees did not seriously begin until after the deportations from France in the summer of 1942. When they did, Spanish officials were careful not to offend the Western powers too much, and it was not clear at all whether fleeing Jews might not be the subject of Western concern.

While cases existed where Jews were returned to the German border patrols, most Jews were not. Men were interned in a very bad camp, Miranda del Ebro, women and children usually in forced residences. From summer 1942 until the liberation of France in August 1944, some 7,500 Jews crossed the Pyrenees and were kept in camps. There was little possibility of making a clear distinction between Jews and other refugees, and the Spaniards were anxious not to antagonize the Western Allies. When in November 1942 the Germans occupied the hitherto free zone in southern France and their patrols started controlling the Spanish border with great strictness, Spain wanted to stop the influx of all refugees. Strong interventions postponed this step, but on 25 March 1943 Spain closed her borders. It took very strong Allied pressure and the personal intervention of Churchill to make the Spaniards rescind their step. Neither the closure nor the revocation of the order had anything to do with the Jews, but rather with the problem of Allied airmen escaping from German-held territory and of Frenchmen who wanted to join de Gaulle's forces.

The one area where Spain had to solve a problem directly concerned with Jews was when the German foreign office demanded that Spain either take back Jews with Spanish citizenship or allow the Nazis to treat them on a par with others, i.e., deport them. This applied to about four thousand individuals, about three thousand of whom lived in France. The German demarche gave Spain until the end of March 1943 to decide. Spain's policy on these Spanish citizens of Jewish descent clearly showed her basic attitude at the time: the government in Madrid prevaricated, discussed, gave orders that were immediately countermanded, and in the end agreed to take back her own Jewish citizens, provided they did not stay in Spain but were moved on to North Africa or elsewhere. In any case, Spain was not willing to pay any money in order to save these few Jewish people. Most of them did not reach Spain, but the lukewarm interest evinced for them by Madrid saved their lives: the Nazis interned them and most of them survived the war. Some were deported to their deaths despite the Spanish passports they held.[47]

What emerges is a cold, calculating posture by the Spanish government, which was pushed into a few half-hearted acts to give aid to a few of their Jewish citizens. Only late in 1944, with the war already practically won by the Allies and Spain surrounded by Allied-controlled territories, did the Spanish government permit itself the humanitarian gesture of declaring its acceptance of a number of Hungarian Jewish children. None of them actually managed to reach Spain. The fable of Spain's great help to the Jews under the Nazi regime is just that—a fable.

This of course does not mean that there were not Spaniards who were deeply affected by what they saw happening to Jews all over Europe. This applies especially to some of the Spanish diplomatic representatives in European cities, who did everything in their power to help Jews. Haim Avni's research points to the fact that although there were practically no Jews in Spain, the traditional enmity to Jews and to Judaism had created a stereotype of Jews in the Spanish mind, which corresponded to rather violent forms of antisemitism in contemporary Europe. Spain saw herself threatened by international Jewry, which was one of the ruling elements in the countries of the democratic West, and which was a traditional enemy of Christianity and of Spain.

In a very moderate and mild way, this same concept was accepted also by Dr. Heinrich Rothmund, head of the Swiss Alien Police, the Swiss official who more than anyone else in Switzerland influenced the policy of his government on the question of European Jews under Nazi rule.

Rothmund also thought that American Jewry wielded a tremendous influence over President Roosevelt. He could not understand why tiny Switzerland, desperately trying to protect its neutrality in the midst of territories controlled by Nazi Germany, should save so many Jews, while American Jewry could not or did not care to use its influence to liberalize American policies. Switzerland had little extra food, it had no natural resources, and its tourist industry was all but dead a a result of the war. Why should it endanger itself by admitting Jews, who were considered by Nazi Germany as that country's worst enemy?

At the outbreak of war, there were some five thousand Jewish refugees in Switzerland, who had escaped from Germany and Austria and had not managed to find other places of refuge before Switzerland was surrounded by the Nazi hordes. Swiss government directives, often echoed in the conservative press, saw the Jews as *wesensfremd,* or essentially foreign. In November 1939 they were explicitly termed "undesirables." Between the summer of 1940 and the summer of 1942, about one thousand such Jewish undesirables were admitted, in line with a regulation that accepted only women, children under sixteen, and men over sixty. The others were returned to the Nazis.

But there was another side to the Swiss tradition, that of providing a haven for genuine refugees and unfortunates. Swiss liberal opinion, and that of a growing number of Protestant pastors, was heard in defense of the right of asylum. It was well understood that this was not an inherent right of the refugee but a right bestowed upon him by the Swiss. Nevertheless, the return of refugees by Swiss guards to Vichyite or German police—a process known as *refoulement*—meant suffering and possible death for the refugees and this went against the grain of a large section of public opinion. Essentially, the argument was between the conservative, largely agricultural cantons in the center of the country and the more urban, liberal cantons on the periphery. Rothmund himself was affected by the wave of liberal opinion, and when this was fortified by the terrible reports about the summer deportations from France, he gave orders in August 1942 to admit refugees from France. His Minister of the Interior promptly countermanded the order. On 13 August, another order signed by Rothmund instructed the border police to admit political refugees only. "Refugees for racial reasons only, for instance Jews, do not count as political refugees." In the course of the next few weeks, pressure and counterpressure produced contradictory and essentially unworkable instructions for the Swiss border police. As a result, thousands were admitted who managed to slip past the French and German patrols. Many, perhaps hundreds, perhaps thousands, were *refoulé* and ended up in Auschwitz. Between August and December 1942, 8,467 Jewish refugees were admitted into Switzerland. By the end of the war, the grand total of Jews admitted during the war into the country was somewhwere near the 21,000 mark. According to my own calculation, at least one fourth of that number again were *refoulé,* mostly to their deaths. The total of all the refugees, including military personnel, who were admitted into Switzerland during the war amounted to 295,381 persons, so that the percentage of the Jews came to less than ten. Included in the number of the Jews were the three trainloads of Jews, two from Budapest via Bergen-Belsen, and one from the Theresienstadt ghetto, who came in the last war year. They had been admitted despite the declaration of Rothmund that Switzerland would only accept Jewish children, or such adults as had relatives in the country; it would also, he said, categorically refuse admission to anyone who had gained access by paying or having had paid for him ransom.

Despite pressure by Swiss liberals, therefore, the number of Jews saved from certain death by taking refuge in the small, neutral country in the middle of Europe, was small indeed, especially when one compares it to the numbers of others, non-Jews, who were saved. Some of these others, no doubt, were also in grave danger; others, one suspects, less so. The difference lay in the fact that every Jew who was identified as such by the Nazis was subject to a death sentence. Seen in that light, the action of the Swiss is commendable, but not impressive. That, indeed, was the reaction of the Swiss themselves, when in the 1950s they conducted an investigation into their government's wartime refugee policy. They drew some practical conclusions as well, as can be seen by their very liberal attitude to persecuted groups and individuals in the postwar era.

In the end, a historian cannot avoid moral problems, nor should he want to do so. You can read all about the silence of the free world while the Jewish people were being gassed and shot and starved to death; books, good books, have been written about it. In confirming this picture, I have tried to point out other things as well: that motivations and actions differed; that one must differentiate between different national traditions, between different political and economic circumstances, between nations conquered by the Nazis and those on the outside, between people and their leaders. My conclusion is that generalizations are easy to utter and much more difficult to defend; that in the darkness of Gentile attitudes to Jews there shone many bright lights. In places where the darkness was black indeed, the lights, though few, shone much brighter. In the end, beyond political and religious convictions, it was basic morality that counted. There were places where it was easier to be a moral person, moral in the sense that when you were challenged with, "thy brother's blood is calling," you answered, "I am here." We have much to learn yet about the Holocaust in this, as well as in other, areas of inquiry. But as we all know, the question is no less important than the answer. We are asking about the human response to human tragedy, about the feeling of community between groups and individuals, about the community of interests between people who care for and respect each other and each other's legitimately different traditions. The Holocaust is a touchstone of such inquiry.

Actually, the topic of this chapter is probably badly phrased. There is no "After." We are living in an age when holocausts are possible; possible but not inevitable. Discussing attitudes and reactions during the Holocaust we have, in fact, explored not just the forties, but the sixties and seventies of this century. We have asked questions about our present and our future. That is the universalist meaning of the Holocaust, precisely because it does not involve an abstraction but a real, living Jewish people, proud of being one of the most ancient and important civilizations on this earth.

Allow me to end this chapter with a story. On my kibbutz there lives a man whom we shall call here Tolek. All he knows about himself is his name. He was born near Cracow, or in Cracow, prior to World War II, and he was three when the war broke out. He was in an orphanage, probably because his father had died and his mother could not support him. A Polish woman took this circumcized man-child to her home and raised him there during the Nazi occupation, in alliance with a Catholic parish priest. When the Nazis came searching Polish homes for hidden Jews, the woman used to hand over Tolek to the priest. Tolek still remembers how, at the age of five and six, he used to assist the priest at Mass, swinging the incense around, walking behind the priest through the church. They survived the war, and when liberation came, the woman took Tolek to a Jewish children's home and said, this is a Jewish child, I have kept him throughout the war, he belongs to your people, take him and look after him. Tolek does not know the name of the Polish woman, nor does he know the name of the priest. There are not very many such women, and there are not very many such priests, and therefore there are not a great many Toleks around. But there are some of each.

4. The Mission of Joel Brand

ON 19 MAY 1944, A GERMAN COURIER PLANE LANDED AT Istanbul. Among the passengers were Joel Brand, member of the underground Jewish Assistance and Rescue Committee at Budapest,[1] and Andor ("Bandi") Grosz (alias Andreas Gyorgy—and several other aliases), also a Hungarian Jew and a triple or quadruple espionage agent and smuggler. Brand was received by members of the Istanbul group of Jewish Agency rescue workers. He had no Turkish visa, and it was Grosz who bailed him out through his local contacts.[2] Reporting to the assembled group of Jewish Agency workers later that day, Brand told them of the mission he had been entrusted with by the head of the Nazi *Sondereinsatzkommando* who had come to Budapest to destroy Hungarian Jewry, Adolf Eichmann. Eichmann, Brand said, had offered to release one million Jews in exchange for goods, such as ten thousand trucks, eight hundred tons of coffee, two hundred tons each of cocoa, sugar, and tea, and two million bars of soap. The story of this famous "trucks for blood" offer is the subject of this chapter.

Who was behind the Nazi offer? What were the motives of those who made it? Was it meant seriously? Would the Nazis actually have released Jews for some kind of payment? What was the reaction of the Allied powers to the offer? What was the reaction of the official Jewish bodies? Was there any realistic chance of the offer being accepted? Nothing came of the offer as it stood—why? A first attempt will be made in this chapter to answer, partly at least, some of these questions. Beyond them lies a major historical and moral problem: could some, or many, European Jews have been saved through the instrumentality of the Brand proposals and, if so, how was that opportunity missed?

Surprisingly, not much has been written as yet on this fantastic episode of the Holocaust. To be sure, all major studies mention it, but no detailed examination has appeared to date.[3] The material is there. The time has come, it seems, to try to evaluate the evidence.

ANTECEDENTS

Who was Joel Brand? Born on 25 April 1906 at Naszod in Transylvania, he grew up at Erfurt in Germany, where his family had moved in 1910 or 1911. He claims to have finished a technical school in 1923, and to have completed his *Abitur,* or matriculation examination.[4] He joined the Communist party, and then traveled, quite possibly as a Comintern agent, to America. He appears to have spent some time in the major American cities. He traveled in the Pacific and the Far East, and spent some time in Latin America. He returned to Germany in about 1927, rejoining his father's firm.[5] According to his cousin, Andreas Biss, Brand became a member of the Thuringian Communist party presidium. The Nazi's accession to power found him in a hospital with a wound inflicted in one of the bloody Nazi-Communist encounters. He was arrested and spent over a year in Nazi prisons. He himself claimed that because of his Hungarian passport (though Naszod had become Romanian in the meantime) he was finally released and expelled from Germany in July or August, 1934.[6]

According to Biss, Brand now found work at Biss's factory. As he was, however, not averse to heavy drinking and did not like hard work, he soon got into trouble and had to leave for Budapest (he was still a Hungarian citizen). At first he took employment in a branch of his father's firm in Hungary, but later he decided to immigrate to Palestine. He joined "Gordonia," a moderate left-wing Zionist youth movement and spent some time on a preparatory farm (*hachsharah*) in order to be entitled to a certificate of immigration to Palestine. In 1935 he married Haynalka (Hansi) Hartmann in what appears to have been at first a marriage of convenience, entered into in order to qualify for the hoped-for Palestine certificate. However, a family was founded, and Hansi Brand developed a shop making knitted gloves. Joel became the buying and selling agent.

Joel Brand became active in the Zionist movement. He became a member of the executive committee of Ihud, the moderate left-wing party connected with the Mapai party in Palestine, and was active in fund-raising.

In July–August 1941, 18,000 Jews, many of whom had been born in Hungary, were expelled by the Hungarian police into Poland, supposedly as "aliens." Of those, close to 16,000 were murdered by ss Obergruppenfuehrer Franz Jaeckeln's *Einsatzgruppe* troops at Kamenets Podolsk on 27 and 28 August 1941.[7] Among those expelled were Hansi Brand's sister and her husband. A coffeehouse acquaintance of Brand's, a Hungarian army intelligence officer, Lieutenant Joszi Krem, agreed to try to bring back Brand's relatives—in return for a handsome payment, of course.[8]

This first contact developed into an ever-expanding activity of saving Hungarian, and later Polish, Jews by bringing them into Hungary, which was until 1944 a relatively safe haven for the Jewish people being murdered by the Nazis all over Europe. With the help of young leaders of Zionist youth movements, mostly people who came into Hungary after fleeing from Slovakia where the deportations to the Polish ghettos and death camps started in March 1942, Brand ran a very efficient organization smuggling Jews across into Hungary. He did so on behalf of Ihud and with the knowledge of the leader of the Hungarian Zionist organization, Otto Komoly.

This is a good point at which to introduce the general background to Brand's work. In 1941, after the annexation of what were formerly parts of Romania, Yugoslavia, and Czechoslovakia to Hungary, there were 725,007 Jews in the country; in addition, there were 61,548 converts to Christianity. Together with other people who were Jewish by Nazi definition, the total must have been somewhat above 800,000. In fact, however, the Jews of Hungary were a declining community, with a low birthrate and a high rate of conversion. In 1930, some 65 percent of the Jews belonged to the so-called neologue, or liberal community, which favored a policy of assimilation with the Magyar nation. Close to 30 percent belonged to the Orthodox group, which was actually no less identified with Hungary in speech and customs, except for the strict observance of Jewish religious tradition. The Orthodox element was strengthened in number by the annexations of 1938 to 1941. The Zionists were opposed by both these major movements; they were but a small minority among Hungarian Jews. With the annexation of parts of Transylvania by Hungary in 1940, the relatively stronger Zionist movement there strengthened the small Hungarian Zionist group somewhat. Dr. Rudolf (Reszoe) Kastner, a gifted journalist from Cluj, settled in Budapest and became the acknowledged leader of the Ihud group and, in effect, Komoly's deputy.[9]

Discrimination against Hungarian Jews had been the

policy of Hungary's authoritarian regime, headed by Admiral Miklos Horthy, since 1919. A racial definition of Jews and a numerus clausus in Hungarian universities (Jewish students could not count more than 6 percent of the study body) dated from 1920, though they were repealed in 1928. Two antisemitic laws of 1938 and 1939 limited the percentage of Jews in most branches of the economy. In the following few years marriages between Jews and Christians were forbidden, the official status of the Jewish religion was denied, and labor battalions were set up for Jews instead of the usual military service. Even before Hungary's entry into the war in the wake of Germany's attack on the Soviet Union, 52,000 Jews were recruited into these battalions, where they were treated with brutality as, more or less, slave laborers. After June 1941, more were recruited, and some 40,000 sent to the Russian front, where only about 25 percent or less survived. The total number of Jewish men serving in these units has been estimated at up to 100,000, but there were probably fewer than that. The absence of most young men of military age from their communities during the deportation period in 1944 had a considerable influence on the reaction of the Jewish masses: no widespread resistance was possible without men aged 18–35.

Brand himself was also threatened with recruitment into these labor battalions, but, like a large number of other young Jews, managed to cheat his way out of the service.[10]

Attempts made to organize the rescue work on a more formal basis dated from December 1941, when Kastner tried to form a respectable aid and rescue committee with the participation of Liberals and Social Democrats, but he failed. Finally, in January 1943, the Assistance and Rescue Committee (called the "Va'adah" in the correspondence) was established in Budapest, with Komoly as chairman, Kastner at his deputy, and Samu (Shmuel) Springmann, Joel Brand, and a few others. A request from the Istanbul group of Jewish Agency emissaries to establish just such a group (February 1943) simply caused the Va'adah to announce its existence to the Jewish bodies in the free world.[11] In the meantime, Springmann, a jeweler by profession, had in October 1942 established a first contact with Istanbul. The courier was Andor ("Bandi") Grosz, who was an agent of the German Abwehr, the military intelligence organization under Admiral Canaris, which stood in opposition to the Hitler regime and was by that time looking for a way to a possible peace. At the same time, Grosz was also in contact with the Hungarian Military Intelligence, as we shall discuss in greater detail later on. Grosz agreed to serve the Va'adah as well, and began delivering letters between Istanbul and Budapest.[12] Brand was responsible for the smuggling of Polish Jews into Hungary; the numbers were limited, but a total of some 2,500 were apparently saved,[13] and this was mostly the work of Brand and his small group of youngsters from the Zionist youth movements.

On 13 March 1944, members of the Abwehr in Budapest, who by that time had established direct contacts with the heads of the Va'adah, announced to them that Jewish matters would now pass from the SS to the army. What lay behind this misinformation, and whether it was intentional or not, has remained a mystery. The next day, however, the Va'adah members were told that the Germans were about to occupy Hungary, and this information reached Istanbul on the seventeenth.[14] On 19 March, the Germans marched in.

RANSOM

In this early period one of the most puzzling problems is the relationship between the Abwehr, the Hungarian Intelligence, and the Va'adah. It must be remembered that in February 1944 Himmler abolished the Abwehr and merged it with his own foreign intelligence organization, the SD, headed by Walter Schellenberg. The Abwehr under Canaris had established its contacts abroad with the clear notion that Germany had lost the war. The SD leadership was well aware of the Abwehr views. But the Abwehr groups abroad had mostly deserted to the Allies; the Abwehr was bankrupt, and no longer much of an opponent even before February. It now seems clear, however, that Schellenberg and his immediate colleagues in fact shared the views of Canaris and his co-conspirators such as Colonel Hans Oster and Dr. Hans von Dehnanyi—Germany was lost and contacts with the Western Allies should be established. It seems that the only issue at stake in Budapest was that the group of Abwehr people there were unaware of the takeover of their organization by Himmler at the end of February, and that they held in their hands a trump card: contacts with Istanbul. The SD would naturally seek to take these contacts from them.

The Abwehr group in Budapest was controlled from the Abwehrstelle IIIF in Vienna, and was headed by a Dr. Josef Schmidt. Other members of this group were Josef (Joszi) Winninger, alias Duftel (or Duft), reportedly of Jewish descent; Rudi Scholz; and a Dr. Rudolf Sedlaczek, a Viennese who was Schmidt's deputy. Some of these men were very unsavory characters, heavy drinkers and blackmailers. Their main contact man with Istanbul, Bandi Grosz, was also their chief contact with the Hungarians and the local Va'adah. When the SS entered Budapest on

19 March, they were therefore most eager to put their hands on these people without destroying the existing ties the Abwehr had established.[15]

During the last weeks before the German occupation, Brand had been the main liaison between the Va'adah and the Abwehr. Now, on 19 March, Winninger and one other man came to his "second home" at the Hotel Majestic in Budapest (he felt unsafe at his "real" home, and he was moving out in any case), and more or less forced him to take refuge with Rudi Scholz in order to escape the ss, who had however managed to arrest Grosz. Brand gave Winninger $8,000 in cash and a gold cigarette case, or according to another account, $20,000, ten to twelve thousand Swiss francs, and fifty to sixty gold coins at $20 each, none of which he saw again. These appear to have been the Va'adah's funds, and not, as Brand claims in his book, his own private property.[16] Grosz later joined him at the Scholz apartment.

A few days after the occupation, Brand was released, and participated at a meeting of the Va'adah. It became clear that with the ss troops there had arrived a special commando under Adolf Eichmann to deal with the Jewish problem. A Judenrat (Jewish Council) was being set up, and it was obvious that the Hungarian Jews would share the fate of Polish Jewry, unless something was done quickly. Kastner, in fact, says that this is what they were told by Winninger.[17]

Could they resist by force? The Istanbul group had demanded of the Va'adah to prepare arms late in 1943. Istanbul also nominated a commander—Moshe (Miklos) Schweiger. Some arms were indeed collected; according to Brand, these amounted to 150 pistols, forty grenades, three rifles, and two machine guns, of which one was serviceable.[18] This was hardly enough to stage a rebellion with, and in any case Schweiger was arrested immediately upon the German conquest, and held at Mauthausen—he was freed by Kastner towards the end of the war.

There seemed to be one viable alternative: to find an SS officer with whom one could discuss some kind of ransom plan. The idea was not as unlikely as it seemed at first; there had been a most important and significant precedent.

In March 1942, the Nazis began deporting Slovak Jews to Poland and death. A group of Jewish leaders from all the various groups and parties, led by Rabbi Michael Dov-Ber Weissmandel and by Mrs. Gizi Fleischmann, came into being, devoted to the idea of trying to save Jews by bribe and ransom. Weissmandel, the son-in-law of the acknowledged leader of ultra-Orthodoxy in Slovakia, Rabbi Shlomo David Halevi Ungar of Nitra, was the unlikely partner in this enterprise with his distant relative, Gizi Fleischmann, who was the head of the Women's Zionist Organization—actually, a ladies' benevolent society. Through the intermediary of a Jewish traitor they contacted Dieter Wisliceny, the SS expert on Jewish affairs attached to the German embassy at Bratislava. In June 1942, they agreed to pay $50,000 to the Nazis, in two equal parts, in return for a cessation of the deportations. The deportations ceased. The "working group," as the Weissmandel-Fleischmann leadership called itself, had difficulties in raising the second half of the payment. Some more transports were sent to Poland; the rest of the ransom was paid, and the deportations ceased, not to be renewed until the autumn of 1944.[19]

It is not quite clear to what extent the cessation of the deportations was the result of the ransom payment or of other factors independent of it. What is perfectly clear is that the "working group" believed that its policy had stopped the deportations. A further approach was therefore made to Wisliceny in November 1942, and a ransom payment offered for the release of all European Jews. This proposal, which came to be known as the "Europa Plan," was to all appearances taken very seriously by the Nazis. Wisliceny went to Berlin to discuss the plan with his superiors—after the war he claimed that he had discussed it with Eichmann—and he came back to Bratislava demanding $2 million in foreign currency, to be paid up after talks on neutral territory. In return, the Nazis would desist from the deportation of West European and Balkan Jewry. These discussions dragged along until August 1943, because Jews in the free world to whom the "working group" turned for the money did not take the German proposal seriously. In any case, there was no money and, even if there were, there was no way of transferring it in contravention of Allied blockade procedures.[20]

What interests us here is: who stood behind these German proposals, and to what extent were the Germans serious? It seems quite clear that Wisliceny received his instructions ultimately from Himmler. It is also clear that it was not the $2 million that were central to the German proposal, but the fact that such money could only be paid as a result of some kind of negotiations. Was Himmler interested, in 1943, after the defeats of the German armies at El Alamein and Stalingrad, in contacts with the West through the Jews? Was he thinking of using his desperate Jewish hostages in an attempt to create such contacts?

Kastner and Komoly were very well aware of all that had transpired in Bratislava. They were in constant touch with Weissmandel and Fleischmann. The "working group" on its part reacted to the occupation of Hungary by contacting Wisliceny—or possibly it was Wisliceny who initiated the contact—and gave the Nazi letters of introduction to three Hungarian Jewish groups: the Orthodox group unter Fülop von Freudiger, leader of an Orthodox Rescue Committee which had been established in 1943 and which, since November 1943, had a working agreement with the Komoly-Kastner group; the official Zionist leadership in Hungary; and the Baroness Edith Weiss.[21]

The Va'adah members were looking for a way to contact Wisliceny. The Abwehr people, maneuvering for a place in the negotiations that would guarantee their own survival, offered to mediate—for a consideration. According to Brand, Winninger and Sedlaczek were to receive 1 percent each of the first bribe of $200,000 that would be offered to Wisliceny, and the whole Abwehr group would get another 10 percent. The Va'adah's stipulation was that the "status quo"—Nazi abstention from ghettoization and deportation—would be maintained in the meantime.[22] If the "status quo" were maintained, the SS would get the $2 million that the Slovak "working group" had originally discussed with Wisliceny.

Obviously, the Va'adah was not so eager now to advance the meeting, because they thought that the SS would now stop their preparations for deportations in expectation of a meeting with the Jews. How much mistaken they were in this hope can be seen from the frantic pace with which Eichmann was pushing towards the destruction of Hungarian Jewry. Ex-Prime Minister Miklos Kallay had found refuge in the Turkish embassy in Budapest. A new government was formed under Döme Sztojay, former Hungarian ambassador in Berlin. Pro-Nazi Minister of the Interior Andor Jaross nominated two antisemitic extremists, Laszlo Endre and Laszlo Baky, as secretaries in his ministry. Negotiations between Eichmann and these Hungarian Nazis were speeded up; on 29 March Jaross suggested the introduction of the yellow star to be worn by all Jews. A Judenrat was set up by Eichmann under Samu Stern, composed largely of docile, frightened men who thought that

if they only behaved quietly and obeyed the orders of the
ss, nothing would happen to them. Wisliceny and Eichmann made speeches on 31 March to the Jewish leaders in
this spirit. On 4 April, Endre prepared the order for the
ghettoization of Jews in the provinces, and this was sent
out to local authorities on the seventh, in full collaboration of course with Eichmann. In the meantime, a large
number of orders were inflicted on the Judenrat and on the
Jewish community generally: curfew, prohibition of
travel, confiscation of banking accounts, confiscation of
property. Complete submission by the Judenrat to all German commands aided in the process. On 15 April, ghettoization began in the Subcarpathian province of Hungary.
There was no sign of any Hungarian resistance to this policy, and a great deal of support for it from the more na-
tionalistic and pro-German elements. The Jews were isolated, cowed, friendless, and disoriented.

The question has been asked whether Hungarian Jews
knew about the destruction process that was by that time
almost completed in large parts of Nazi-controlled Europe.
The additional question has been asked why the Jewish
leadership in Hungary, if it knew of the destruction process did not warn Hungarian Jewry, and did not encourage
massive flight into Romania or attempts to hide in
Hungary. It would seem that such questions are based on
a misunderstanding of the situation. Hungarian Jewish
leaders, including leaders of the neologue and Orthodox
communities, certainly had full information of the Nazi
war of murder against the Jews. This information had
been there since 1942, if not earlier. It had not been confined to the leadership. Thousands of Slovak Jews had fled
to Hungary in 1942, including Polish Jews who had managed to flee from Poland to Slovakia earlier on. Twenty-
five hundred additional Polish Jews had entered Hungary
between 1942 and 1944, had dispersed in Hungarian

towns, and had lived among Hungarian Jews. The Allied radio broadcasts concerning the mass destruction of the Jews had been beamed, in Hungarian, to Hungary since the end of 1942, and been listened to all over the country. Thousands of Hungarian soldiers on leave from the eastern front had told their stories in their home towns. A few thousand Jewish labor battalion members had been re- leased in 1943, and had told their harrowing stories in their homes—they too had seen the mass destruction in the east. To say that Hungarian Jewry had to rely on their leadership for information regarding the "Final Solution" is to misread the whole historical process. This mistake has at its root the confusion between "information" and "knowledge." The information was there all the time, including information regarding the ways in which the Nazis were misleading and fooling their victims. The point is that this information was rejected, people did not *want* to know, because knowledge would have caused pain and suffering, and there was seemingly no way out. In the Judenrat building itself, an office was established for con- tacts with the provincial communities, later ghettos. From this office, members of Zionist youth movements were sent out to warn the provincial Jews of impending destruc- tion. Not only did their warnings go unheeded, but in many instances they were thrown out of the communities by the local leaderships for spreading panic.[23]

It seems doubtful today, protestations to the contrary notwithstanding, whether the Jewish masses in Hungary were prepared to risk flight to Romania or to make at- tempts at hiding. Obviously, only those communities that were very near the Romanian border stood any chance at all for the first alternative, and the second was barred by the behavior of the Hungarian people. The absence of most young men who were doing their service with the labor battalions also played a part. But in the light of the general situation it seems questionable whether the Jewish leadership and the Jewish people were psychologically capable of absorbing as knowledge what they had at their disposal as information: the fact of the Nazi desire to murder all of them. The Va'adah, it must be remembered, was acting within that somber framework.

The date of the first meeting with Wisliceny, at Winninger's house, is not quite established. From internal evidence it would appear to have taken place on about 29 March.[24] Kastner and Brand were met by Dr. Schmidt and Winninger of the Abwehr, Wisliceny of the Eichmann commando, and ss Hauptsturmfuehrer Erich Klausnitzer, who later turned out to be a member of the SD. This participation of the SD in the very first meeting is significant. The SD under Schellenberg was represented in the new postoccupation setup in Budapest by ss Hauptsturmfuehrer Otto Clages (or Klages),[25] who was Eichmann's equal and in certain matters apparently superior. Both Eichmann and Klages were nominally under the Higher ss and Police Leader Dr. Otto Winkelmann, and in political matters had to take into account the opinion of Dr. Edmund Veesenmayer, the German ambassador who now became the de facto governor of Hungary, and who also held an ss rank. Through Klages and Schellenberg, the contacts led to Himmler, just as they obviously led to the same place through Wisliceny and Eichmann.

The two Va'adah representatives asked for a stop to executions of Hungarian Jews in Hungary; for an agreement not to ghettoize the Jews; not to deport them; and for permission for those of them having entrance permits to foreign countries, to emigrate. As to Wisliceny's answer, there are some discrepancies between Brand and Kastner, but they both agree that Wisliceny promised there would be no deportations, no ghettoization, and that emigration was possible, but only on a large scale. According to Kastner, Wisliceny promised that the "substance" of Hungarian Jewry would be preserved; when pressed to define what he meant by that, he answered that he meant "the biological base," and did not elaborate any further.[26]

On the monetary side, Wisliceny agreed to receive a down payment of $200,000, in Hungarian currency, but he warned that the total sum of $2 million might well be insufficient, and that he would have to take advice from Berlin on this point. According to Kastner's report, the Jewish representatives declared that they could only get the required sum (presumably the overall payment, not the down payment) provided the Jewish organizations abroad accepted the German demand.[27] Neither Kastner nor Brand repeated this statement in the other testimonies they gave, but it stands to reason that that is what they said—how indeed could the money be obtained (in dollars!) unless there was contact abroad? If this is what they told Wisliceny, then the subsequent contacts between Eichmann and Brand are much easier explained.

The testimonies of the participants diverge on what happened now. Kastner says that the money was raised by Samu Stern, and that only a first payment of 3 million pengö (out of 6.5 million, the equivalent of $200,000) could be mustered for the first subsequent meeting, at which Hermann Krumey and Otto Hunsche, two other Nazis of the Eichmann commando, appeared instead of Wisliceny. Brand repeats the same story in his book, but in his testimony to the British he says that they already paid Wisliceny an advance payment at the first meeting, and that he had a separate, second meeting with Wisliceny on 2 April, at which another part of the bribe was paid. Brand says that he asked the Nazis why they had not kept the promise not to establish ghettos, and that he submitted a memorandum on emigration. He does not mention that Kastner was present at the meeting. The fact that the ghettoization did not start before 15 April seems to discredit Brand's first story, although it is the earliest full testimony we have.[28] The meeting with Krumey and Hunsche occurred, according to this source, on 9 April.

At the next meeting, with Krumey and Hunsche—on 21 April, according to Kastner—another 2.5 million pengö were paid; the Jews had been unable to pay the additional million. The Nazis were disgusted. Was this the way to keep a gentlemen's agreement? They stonewalled on the question of ghettoization and deportation. Emigration was possible, but only on a large scale. The outstanding million pengö were only paid in early May. The Abwehr people now informed Kastner and Brand that deportation had been decided upon, and that the only hope for a stay of the execution was to prepare large sums of money. It was impossible to obtain a confirmation of this information from the Hungarians or the SS, but the lightning speed of the ghettoization was proof enough. The 21 April meeting was the end of phase one in the Brand story.[29]

TRUCKS FOR BLOOD

What happened afterwards has been told a number of times, though again there are slight discrepancies. According to Brand, on 25 April Winninger arranged for Brand to be picked up and brought to Eichmann, at the latter's demand. It seems that Eichmann offered him one million Jews—according to another version, all the European Jews—in return for goods, "for example—lorries. I could imagine one lorry for a hundred Jews, but that is only a suggested figure." Eichmann asked Brand what kind of Jews he wanted. Young men? Women? Children? Old people? Brand answered he wanted all of them, and when asked where he suggested to go to negotiate a deal of that sort, he answered that he preferred Istanbul, because it was there that the representation of Palestinian Jews could help him contact the Western Allies. "In reference to the vehicles, Eichmann also said they would be used on the Eastern Front, and not in the West."[30]

A second meeting with Eichmann took place a few days later. Two important things happened there. First, Veesenmayer was present. In other words, whoever was behind the German offer was making sure he had the support, at least partly, of the Foreign Office, or at least that part of it which was allied to the SS, as Veesenmayer undoubtedly was. The other matter that becomes clear is that the Germans had no immediate, concrete proposal to make. The demand for trucks was at first not as definite as later literature was to make out. What stood out immediately, however, was the crude attempt to indicate to the Western Allies that the SS did not want to fight against them; the offer was phrased so that the intention to try to cause a division among the anti-Nazi allies was obvious.

Brand told his British interrogators that after this second meeting he discussed the Nazi proposal a number of times with Krumey, Eichmann's aide, who elaborated on the Germans' need for machines and machine tools, for raw materials, for leather and hides, and so on.

A third meeting between Brand and Eichmann took place on 8 or 10 May.[31] At this meeting Eichmann, in a dramatic gesture, threw at Brand letters and monies that had been sent to the Va'adah from Switzerland and had been caught by the Nazis. A sum of $32,750 and very confidential and compromising letters were handed him, the letters apparently without having been opened first.[32] The letters and the money were given to the SD by Grosz. How did Grosz come into their possession? Very simply. The batch had been brought from Switzerland to the Swedish Military Attache in Budapest, who could not find Brand, and decided to give the material to Grosz, whom he knew to be in touch with Brand. The SD had gotten wind of the fact that the Swedes were looking for Grosz, had arrested him, and forced him to receive the letters and the money and hand both over to them.[33]

Why did Eichmann and Klages hand over the material to Brand? Obviously, what was involved in Nazi eyes was more than some small illegal activities of the Va'adah; they had to convince Brand that they meant their offer seriously, if he was to succeed in his mission. Of course, being Nazis, they demanded 10 percent for Grosz—in actual fact Grosz only got a fraction of that, and the SD men pocketed the rest. Their whole behavior in this matter leaves open the possibility that they might have received an order from Berlin of how to handle the packet from Switzerland. The tone of the conversation, if one is to believe Brand, was fairly typical of Nazi attitudes. When Brand expressed doubts as to his ability to produce goods, Eichmann answered "that the international Jews control the world; they control every British and American official, so that they could lay their hands on anything they wanted."[34] When Brand was asked how long he expected to stay abroad and he answered, about two or three weeks, Eichmann said that he would lay down no definite time limits, but that the negotiations had to be concluded quickly. That was in line with what Wisliceny told Kastner on 25 April: the deportation of all Hungarian Jews had been decided upon, and Brand's mission was the only way of rescue. "Do everything that this journey does not end negatively, and try to achieve at least the partial satisfaction of the German demands; you may win some time by doing so."[35] That, at least, is the way Kastner has reported the conversation. Something similar may have been said—Wisliceny, like many other Nazis, was trying to prepare an alibi for himself—but Kastner was to accuse Brand of failing the Va'adah in his mission, and he may have embellished Wisliceny's utterance to prepare his readers for the argument that Hungarian Jews were killed because of the failure of Brand to return to Hungary.

The handing over to the Va'adah of mail intercepted by the SD was repeated on 14 May, in a direct encounter between Klages and Brand. This time it was a matter of $50,000 and 270,000 Swiss francs, and of letters calling upon the Jews to get in touch with members of the Social Democratic and Liberal Hungarian underground. A horrified Brand thanked his stars that the SD had apparently again not opened the letters, and paid the demanded 17.5 percent of the money to Grosz.[36]

A fourth and last meeting between Brand and Eichmann took place, apparently, on Tuesday, 16 May.[37] Present were Winkelmann and Veesenmayer, as well as Krumey, so that this was definitely a top-level meeting. The demand for trucks was put more firmly, and it was stated they should be properly winterized, and equipped with trailers and accessories. Again he was asked how long his mission would take him, and he replied a week or two, unless he had to go to Palestine. According to Brand, Eichmann replied, "Good. But be as quick as possible."

At the second meeting Eichmann had declared that if an agreement in principle were reached, he would let a first batch of Jews out. In his talk with Ira Hirschmann on 22 June 1944 Brand stated that Eichmann had promised that "he would let out at first a certain number, ten, twenty, fifty thousand Jews, and for this reason alone it would have been a great thing."[38] In Brand's book, this became a promise to release 100,000 Jews as a first move and to blow up the gassing installations at Auschwitz. In his testimony at the "Kastner trial" and again in his testimony at the Eichmann trial he repeated these statements.[39] Eichmann himself gave a different version of what transpired. In the Sassen interview he stated that a "basic objective of

Reichsfuehrer Himmler [was] to arrange if possible for a million Jews to go free in exchange for 10,000 winterized trucks, with trailers, for use against the Russians on the Eastern Front. . . . I said at the time 'when the winterized trucks with trailers are here, the liquidation machine in Auschwitz will be stopped.' "[40] In the light of the available evidence, one can assume that some kind of an offer was made to Brand that a token number of Jews would be released if the German offer were accepted in principle. Eichmann may have said that if the whole deal went through, he would have Auschwitz dismantled. It is not likely that he was going to do that—or say he would do that—on the strength of an agreement in principle alone.

The Jews that were to be freed would not be allowed to go to Palestine, but to the West, via Spain. "The Germans did not wish to antagonize the Arabs by sending too many Jews to Palestine."[41]

To sum up: in a number of discussions, Brand was offered the release of a large number of Jews against goods. At first vague, the demand later crystallized into a desire for ten thousand trucks, quantities of other goods, and a crude message to the Allies that Germany was ready for cooperation with them against the Russians.

We must now turn to another aspect of the story: the elimination of the Abwehr by the SD. In this connection, the personality of Bandi Grosz becomes central.

Grosz was born in 1905 in Bergeszaz in Hungary. In 1930, he was convicted of a customs offense, and got into further trouble with the law as a result of his attempts to escape from the consequences of his conviction. He became a carpet smuggler and was caught in 1934, but managed by various ruses to postpone punishment until 1941. In that year, he was sentenced to one and one-half years in prison, but again managed to postpone the execution of the sentence. In his flight from the law, he took refuge with the German Abwehr branch in Stuttgart, and did some economic espionage work for the Germans in Switzerland, in 1942. In June 1942 Grosz started to work for Richard Klatt (Kauders) of the German Air Force Intelligence in Sofia, who appears to have been in touch with the Soviets. Slowly disentangling himself from the Stuttgart Abwehr, Grosz began working for the Hungarian Military Intelligence from August 1942. Lieutenant Colonels Antal Merkly, Otto Hatz (the Hungarian military attache at Sofia and Istanbul), and Garzoly belonged to the anti-Nazi wing in the Hungarian army, which wanted to establish contacts with the Allies in order to disengage Hungary from her German alliance. Grosz undertook some smuggling missions to Sofia, working both for Klatt and for the Hungarians. He was to claim later that a number of German agents were expelled from Hungary due to his activity. Using two other agents as subcontractors, Grosz began, from October 1942 on, to transfer letters to Istanbul, and letters and money back to Budapest, for the Zionists. He was persuaded to do this by Shmuel (Samu) Springmann, who later became the treasurer of the Va'adah. From March 1943 on, the date of his own first visit to Istanbul, he became the main courier for the Zionists.

In Istanbul, Grosz contacted British and American Intelligence officers (he was in touch with the Poles as well). These contacts were expanded during his trips to Istanbul in April and May 1943. From Teddy Kollek, who was then one of the Jewish Agency rescue workers in Istanbul, he received in May a letter from an American Intelligence officer by the name of Schwarz for Fritz Laufer in Budapest. Laufer—alias Schroeder, alias Ludwig Mayer—possibly a half-Jewish emigrant from Czechoslovakia, was under Klausnitzer, who served as head of Abwehrstelle III,

Prague. The fact that the United States Intelligence was in touch with the Abwehr at that stage would tend to fortify the assumption that Grosz, the courier, was of some importance to the Germans.

Other German agents entered the picture as well: Popescu and Winninger, of the Budapest branch of Abwehrstelle IIIF, Vienna, among others. They, too, performed services for the Istanbul rescue team, but they were dependent on Grosz for their contacts with the Allies. Springmann in Budapest maintained contact with neutral couriers as well, but the Abwehr people, now working with and through Grosz, became central to the contacts maintained between the Va'adah and Istanbul. In Istanbul, only Menahem Bader of the rescue team suggested that the contact with the Germans be broken off. Ehud Avriel and Teddy Kollek, who were responsible for contacts between the team and the Allied Intelligence services, disagreed because they knew that their service friends needed the German Abwehr couriers.

The Americans tried to plant a radio at the Hungarian Military Intelligence center, and entrusted the radio to Grosz, who gave it to Hatz in Budapest. But apparently Hatz either gave the game away to the Germans, or they got wind of it in some other way. However, Hatz apparently was received by Admiral Wilhelm Canaris, chief of the Abwehr, and discovered that there was common ground between the political views of anti-Nazis in the intelligence services of Hungary and Germany. Springmann was released by the Va'adah from his tasks after a breakdown, and permitted to use a certificate for Palestine; he arrived in Istanbul in February 1944 accompanied by Grosz. Grosz now contacted his friends of the Allied services and expounded on the relationship between the Hungarians and the Abwehr. The Americans tried to introduce more radio sets to Hungary, first via Grosz and then via

Hatz, who was in Istanbul at the time, but it appears that Hatz was afraid of being caught and nothing came of it.

After Springmann's departure, Brand took over the task of maintaining contact with the various couriers and, mainly, with the Abwehr. He got to know Schmidt, Winninger, Scholz, and Sedlaczek, and thus became somewhat of a competitor to Grosz, with whom he had a long-standing acquaintance.

By the time the Germans occupied Hungary, the small-time crook and smuggler, Andor "Bandi" Grosz, had become an important liaison man of Hungarian, German, and Allied Intelligence services.[42] Unknown to him, the SS had taken over the Abwehr organization while he was in Istanbul on his next to last journey there, in February 1944. From later developments it becomes clear that Klausnitzer and Laufer of the Prague Abwehr were speedily integrated into the SD, whereas the Budapest branch of the Vienna Abwehr, under Schmidt, tried to maintain an independent position or, perhaps, tried to bargain for a significant position within the new setup. Their trump card was their courier contacts with Istanbul, and their anchorman was Bandi Grosz.

After the occupation of Hungary, Grosz was arrested by Klausnitzer, and then handed over to the Schmidt group. It seems clear from his account that they tried to blackmail him to give them all the possible information about his contacts in Istanbul, apart of course from giving them access to the Zionist funds. Grosz returned to his Hungarian friends, Hatz, Lieutenant Bagyonyi, and a man by the name of Köves, in order to protect himself from the different German groups.

There is no way of finding out the precise sequence of events leading to the arrest of the Budapest Abwehr group and the addition of Grosz to the Istanbul mission. There are three accounts by Brand—in his interrogation by the British, and two separate ones in the Hebrew and German (and English) versions of his book—and one by Grosz in his interrogation by the British. They all diverge on points of substance as well as on points of detail. In addition, the account by Biss, Brand's cousin, in whose apartment the meetings of the Va'adah took place, and by Kastner, diverge from the other four accounts. Yet a careful comparison between all these accounts points to some general conclusions. First, Grosz, who realized that the SD now ruled in the murky world of German Intelligence, and who had a grudge against the Abwehr in any case, did his best to compromise the Schmidt group and get them arrested, which in fact occurred around 7 May. Obviously, once Grosz had gone over to the SD, Klages, Klausnitzer, and Laufer no longer needed the Schmidt group. In order to justify their removal, Laufer needed some corroborative evidence, and he appears to have obtained it from Brand, who, too, had a grudge against the Abwehr people. Second, Grosz was very eager to accompany Brand on his mission to Istanbul, of which he had originally heard from Winninger. Winninger himself wanted to accompany Brand, and that of course was another good reason for Grosz to want to get rid of him. Grosz managed to blackmail a reluctant Brand to put in a good word for him with Krumey, presumably for Eichmann, who at first rejected the idea. From the context of the testimonies it may be safely concluded that Eichmann was forced into taking Grosz by the SD, headed by Klages. The reason for this is not far to seek: Grosz's value lay in his contacts with the Allies. The innocent Brand could not be trusted with an intelligence mission on behalf of the SD, but Grosz, precisely because of his low character, could. The opportunity was too good to miss. Eichmann must have understood the nature of the Grosz mission, and that would explain his reluctance. But orders were orders, and Klages gave them. Grosz was added to the mission.

There was one further obstacle. The Va'adah was less than happy with the idea of Brand going to Istanbul. The idea of Grosz accompanying him made them wince.[43] In addition, Kastner had his contacts with the Hungarians, and now that Grosz had become an agent of the SD only, it was Kastner who might betray the whole story of the Eichmann offer and the journey to Istanbul to the Hungarians. The SS were going to sell Jews for goods, and make contact with the Allies in Istanbul, whereas the Hungarians were to be left out in the cold. Kastner had to be prevented from making contact with them, if the mission was to produce results for the SS. Grosz, even Brand, may have indicated to the SS that Kastner was in their way. In any case, Kastner was arrested on 10 May, and put out of harm's way until Brand and Grosz were safely spirited away.[44]

The two emissaries went to Vienna on 17 May, but it was not easy to get exit permits. These were a matter for the German Foreign Office, and the SS was in some trouble with Ribbentrop. Contrary to legend, Nazi Germany was an unsuccessful totalitarian state, in that it constituted, in many of its aspects, a conglomeration of feudal fiefs engaged in continual internecine warfare, though lorded over by the unquestioned authority of a charismatic leader. In that context Veesenmayer could be in on the mission, while Veesenmayer's chief, Ribbentrop, might be opposed. In the end, visas were obtained to exit Germany and transit Bulgaria, but not to enter Turkey. The two were put on a plane all the same, and reached Istanbul, as we have seen, on the nineteenth.

Brand had not asked the Germans for a visa, because he was sure that the Jewish Agency people would obtain one for him in Istanbul. He obviously had no conception at all of the absolute powerlessness of the Jewish people during the Holocaust. Influenced as he was by the fact that he had been living in a Nazi-controlled world, he had absorbed some of the assumptions on which the Nazis acted, and these included the idea of the control the Jews supposedly exercised over the Allied nations and, indeed, the whole world.

By a tremendous effort, the Jewish Agency group had in fact obtained a Turkish entry permit, but it was issued in the name of Joel Brand, whereas Brand had come on a German passport issued for Eng. Eugen Band. The visa was useless.

ISTANBUL

After arrival, and after the first long sessions with the rescue team, Brand wanted to go on to Palestine. There he would meet with the Agency leaders; but the Istanbul group—Chaim Barlas, Venia Pomerantz, Menahem Bader, Zeev Schind, Akiva Levinsky, Ehud Ueberall (Avriel)—persuaded him not to do so. Instead, they were going to see Laurence A. Steinhardt, the American ambassador at Ankara. Venia Pomerantz left on 22 May for Palestine to report to Shertok, head of the Agency's political department. On 23 May, Brand and Barlas were to leave for Ankara. According to the story in Brand's book, they were told at the railway station that the Turkish police were looking for him because he had no valid visa for staying in the country. According to his testimony to the British, he went to the police station to apply for a travel permit to Ankara, and it was then discovered he had no visa.[45] What happened afterwards is again unclear in detail, because Brand's testimonies conflict. But his testimony to the British as well as a contemporary letter written by Bader to Pomerantz[46] enable us to reconstruct the situation. From 23 May to 26 May, Brand was allowed to stay in the hotel under a mild kind of house arrest. He received guests and held discussions, but was confined to the hotel. The Turkish authorities had decided to expel both him and Grosz back to Hungary. They were apparently willing to provide them with transit visas to Bulgaria, but not more than that. On 25 May the Turks finally decided, despite interventions on the part of the Barlas group, to expel the two, but the expulsion was to take place three days later. There was apparently another Turkish decision on the twenty-sixth, this time at Cabinet level. Brand was under the impression that the British had intervened in order to demand this Turkish step; but it is unclear what actually motivated the Turks—it could well have been a desire to avoid complications that would compromise their neutrality. On the other hand, Grosz has said that it was the German ambassador, Franz von Papen, who demanded that the Turks expel them to Hungary. This may well have been the case, given the enmity between Ribbentrop and Himmler.[47]

What happened next has become a major bone of contention, not only in historical interpretation, but in Jewish and Israeli politics. Brand was to claim that he was forced into agreeing to go to British-controlled Syria on his way to Palestine rather than return to Hungary as he demanded. After a series of contorted motions in Istanbul, Grosz, who Brand said was a Gestapo agent sent along as his watchdog, decided to hand himself over to the British on 1 June. Brand had hoped to meet with Moshe Shertok (Sharett) in Istanbul, but Shertok cabled that he had not received a visa. The Istanbul Agency group had then forced him into agreeing to go to Syria himself on 5 June. They must have known that he would be arrested there by the British. He was, and that precluded his succeeding in his mission. Had he returned to Budapest, he might have saved many Jewish lives. The awesome responsibility for this failure, he claimed, lay with the Jewish Agency, the left-oriented leadership of the Zionist movement, and the British. Two representatives of the Zionist Right and the Orthodox Agudat Israel, Eri Jabotinsky and Ya'akov Griffel, had warned him on the railway station in Ankara, on his way to the Syrian border, but Avriel, his companion and guide, had disregarded all the warnings.

This version of what happened was first put over by a clever lawyer, Shmuel Tamir, in the so-called "Kastner trial" in 1954. At a time when the Right in Israeli politics was fighting its political battles with the Labor government, Tamir was clearly trying to discredit some of the major Labor figures as well as some of the minor ones by presenting them as willing or unwilling stooges of the British. The British, in Tamir's scenario, had seen to it that Shertok should not get his Turkish visa, and then had engineered the handing over of Brand to them, in order not to have to negotiate seriously regarding the Brand mission. They did not want to have a million Jews on their hands. They did not want to save Jews.[48]

Brand's books appeared after the trial, and there he repeated what he told Tamir: "I told Barlas that I do not want to travel (to Syria), but that I want to ask the German mission (in Istanbul) to return to Budapest."[49] Was there a British-Zionist conspiracy to prevent Brand from returning to Hungary? Were lives lost because he did not return?

Fortunately we have some contemporary evidence to go on. On 27 May, Bader sent a private letter to Pomerantz in Palestine, in which he described the events of the past few days. He sent a second letter on 10 June, after Brand had left. On that same date, Shertok met with Brand in Aleppo, and wrote down what Brand told him. And on 22 June, Ira Hirschmann interviewed Brand at length in

Cairo. What emerges from a comparison of these sources is a somewhat different story from the one described above. In his first letter, a shocked and desperate Bader wrote that on the following night (i.e., the twenty-eighth/twenty-ninth, after the grace of three days had run out) "they will be led to the border." He had cabled to Budapest in the hope that perhaps they might succeed in preventing them being killed immediately on the border as Jews with German travel documents being returned to German-controlled territory. "With lightning speed the feeling is confirmed that we had from the beginning: that we are in the presence of people condemned to death." It was obvious, according to Bader, that Joel must have thought, how will you handle this tremendous burden of my mission, if you are incapable of obtaining for me a travel permit to Ankara? Brand handed over to Bader his personal testament. They were trying desperately to prevent Brand's expulsion to Hungary, and they had appealed to the British to let Brand go to Palestine, though they knew that meant "that Brand's family would be burnt at the stake." They had obtained a letter from the British asking the Turks to expel the two emissaries to Palestine rather than return them to Hungary, but the British had intentionally failed to state that the two were Jews, and the Turks replied that the two would not be permitted to go to British-controlled territory, but would be handed over to the Germans. When asked by the Agency representative, the British officer replied that "they would not give the two a letter confirming that they were Jews, they had their reasons for it, and the Jews had no business to find out what they were." Barlas then approached Steinhardt to persuade the British to grant the two the required letter, and in the end the British relented. But the Turkish police would not listen. Brand was going to be expelled to German territory.[50]

In his second letter, Bader said that as they had to try to prevent Brand's murder in Budapest, they formulated a fictitious formal agreement between the Istanbul rescue team and Brand, bearing the date of 29 May, which Brand could show to Eichmann on his return. In effect, the document promised the Germans a ransom payment of one million Swiss francs a month in return for the cessation of deportation. In return for permitting the emigration of each thousand Jews to Palestine, the Germans would get $400,000; for each thousand Jews to Spain, one million francs. In return for permitting the supply of camps and ghettos, the Germans would receive the equivalent of the amounts sent, of the same goods, for themselves. German plenipotentiaries would be expected to meet with persons from the Allied side who were now on their way to Istanbul (Ira Hirschmann and Shertok were meant). Grosz, Bader said in the letter, was still trying to persuade the rescue team to send them both to Palestine, but it was now clear that both had to return to Budapest. They had another stay of the execution. On the night of 29/30 May, Bader spent many hours trying to convince Brand that he had to accept his fate and go back. "At last, after hours of struggling, he accepted very quietly the decision that they had to return." On the thirtieth, therefore, Brand in his turn tried to persuade Grosz to return, because it was obvious to everyone that they could not send Brand without Grosz. Up until that time it was clear that the Turks were insisting on their return in any case. But on that day the Turks agreed to send them to Palestine. On the thirty-first the passports were sent to the British consulate for visas to Palestine.[51]

The story up to that point is, as we see, quite different from the postwar version: the British strenuously resisted the idea of accepting the two in their territory; Brand had no wish to go back without a definite agreement regarding his mission, which could not be obtained in the absence of higher authorities from Istanbul; the Istanbul Agency group, on the other hand, did not wish to send Brand to Palestine in defiance of Turkish and British wishes, and thought that he had to accept the idea of returning to Budapest with just a flimsy piece of paper signed by the Istanbul group, in the hope of fooling the Nazis and perhaps alleviating the situation.

Two further questions have to be answered. Did Brand know of the mass deportations that had started on 14 May, from the provinces of Hungary to Auschwitz? Yes, he knew. In his interrogation he stated that "he had received information that on Monday (14 May) mass deportations had recommenced."[52] In his later testimonies—in his book, at the Kastner trial—he even claimed to have known that twelve thousand people a day were being shipped to Auschwitz. He may possibly have received that information while in Istanbul, because the rescue team there received desperate pleas from Weissmandel in Slovakia, who saw the trains pass through Slovak territory and reported all the details to Istanbul and Switzerland. The only conclusion Brand could draw from all this was that the Nazis were not waiting for his return. In other words, if he did not come back with something very real in his hands, it was most unlikely that he could help stop the carnage. It would appear that that was a major consideration determining Brand's behavior. Indeed, when this factor is considered, his opposition to returning to Hungary empty-handed, or very nearly so, becomes perfectly understandable.

Another factor, however, has to be considered as well. Shertok was trying to receive a visa to go to Turkey. The High Commissioner in Palestine, Sir Harold MacMichael, claimed he did everything in his power to obtain the visa for Shertok. In fact, in his report to London on 26 May, he said that "Shertok is proceeding to Istanbul as soon as he can (i.e., probably within a few days) for an . . . elucidation of the facts and will report to H. M. Ambassador, Angora."[53] The British embassy in Ankara could not obtain the required Turkish permit. According to Shertok, the High Commissioner cabled the embassy that if Shertok's visa were not received on 30 May, he would send Shertok nevertheless, without a visa. A place was prepared for Shertok on a courier plane leaving for Turkey, but at the last minute a cable from Ankara demanded that Shertok should not come under any circumstances, unless he had a visa.[54] Tamir's later construction appears to have been based on the "diabolical interpretation of history" (Koestler).

On 31 May, Shertok cabled Istanbul that he had no visa, but that Brand should not leave Istanbul until Shertok managed to see him there. The cable was sent not only in Shertok's name, but in that of MacMichael as well.[55] But the two representatives of the British consulate in Istanbul with whom the rescue team had been in touch declared that the journey could not wait, and both had to go to Syria. Grosz now was pressing for all he was worth to leave for British-held territory. He had not fulfilled his mission, he said. He could not return; and without his returning, Brand was doomed to death if he went back alone. Brand became convinced that Grosz was right. So were the Agency people. Nevertheless, in accordance with Shertok's wish, Brand was to wait a few more days in the hope that Shertok would arrive in the meantime. Grosz was permitted to go on 1 June. But Shertok did not come. There was no way out: "there was no way but to have Joel and Ehud (Avriel) travel to you. This decision was dictated by logic, the past which had made Bandi a go-between in an affair we did not believe in at first . . . the refusal of Joel to return alone to those who will interpret Bandi's ab-

sence as treason and flight or kidnapping—and by the
silence of Budapest" (Bader had sent the "agreement" of
29 May to Budapest, but had received no answer—no
wonder, because Hansi Brand and Kastner had in the
meantime been arrested by the Hungarians).[56]

On 7 June, Brand reached Aleppo. He met with Shertok there on the tenth, and was then spirited away to
Cairo. Did the Agency group not suspect that this was
what would happen? In his testimony at the "Kastner
trial," Avriel claimed that he had received a British promise that Brand would be free to return to Turkey and
Hungary.[57] This is confirmed by Shertok,[58] who protested
this breach of promise to MacMichael. Brand was aware of
all this. Did he, then, regret his decision not to return to
Hungary from Istanbul but to go on to Syria? In a moment of truth, after his release by the British, he answered
a direct question by Ira Hirschmann on this score: "He
stated that after the Turks had arrested him . . . he was
given the choice of returning to Hungary, but had he done
so it would have been interpreted as a definite refusal by
the Allies of his proposals, and he saw only dangers of additional reprisals from this eventuality. Now Brand con-
tends that even in spite of the great trials occasioned by
his incarceration, he made the right decision; that at least
he accomplished something with the cessation of the deportations and the 1,700 refugees who did come through
Hungary." Which sounds fair enough. In 1954, and afterwards, then, Brand was lying. Bader and Avriel were
telling the truth. One had better not say anything about
Tamir.[59]

One further puzzle remains in relation to the actual
terms of the Nazi offer. In his cable of 26 May, Mac-
Michael told the British government that Brand would
have to return within fourteen days after his arrival in Is-

tanbul. But, he added, the "terms of negotiations can be prolonged if evidence is forthcoming that [the] scheme is being earnestly considered in high Allied quarters." [60] This is not quite the same as Brand's testimony at the Eichmann trial, where he declared that Eichmann had agreed to hold back the deportees for a week or two and not send them to Auschwitz but to Austria and Slovakia, where he would "keep them on ice"; but he could not wait longer and Brand had to hurry back with his answer. [61] A similar story appears in Brand's book, at the "Kastner trial," and in the accounts by Kastner and others. On the strength of these versions Brand accused the British and, by implication at least, the Jewish authorities as well, of responsibility for the continued murder of Hungarian Jewry because he was not sent back in time. Similarly, Biss and Kastner in their desperation also believed Brand to be responsible, at least in part, for the failure to rescue large numbers of people by going off to Syria instead of returning in time.

It was of course obvious to Brand, as well as to Kastner and Biss, that if Eichmann had said that he would temporarily save the lives of the deportees for the first fortnight by sending them to Austria and Slovakia, he had failed to keep his promise. Later on, 15,000 Hungarian Jews were indeed sent to Strasshof in Austria in order to work there, but the East Hungarian Jews who were the first victims of Eichmann's policies were sent off straight to Auschwitz. There is also no doubt that Brand felt a tremendous responsibility with regard to his mission, and that he wanted to return to Hungary, after seeing Shertok and other leaders, Jewish and Allied, in the free world, with some kind of an answer that would satisfy the Nazis and save Jewish lives. This emerges quite clearly from Shertok's account of his talk with Brand at Aleppo on 10 June.

But in his interrogation by the British as well as in his interview on 22 June with Hirschmann Brand quite explicitly denied that Eichmann had ordered him to return within a fortnight. He had no reason to deny any such order if it had been given, because if he told his interrogators that unless he returned within a given time the lives of hundreds of thousands would be lost, he would have strengthened the case he was making in all the rest of his answers. But Eichmann had said, according to Brand, that he "was not to hurry back but must settle the business." On another occasion, Brand said, he had stated that "he [Brand] might have to go to Palestine. Laufer reiterated Eichmann's reply that he would set no time limit, but that Brand must be as quick as possible."[62] We see again that Brand was twisting the facts in order to suit the developing situation when he claimed, years later, that he had to return within fourteen days. It is highly unlikely that he did this out of bad faith. What is much more likely is that he indeed was acting out of a great sense of urgency, that he knew he must return soon if his mission was to have any success at all, but that as time went on he distorted Eichmann's and Laufer's words somewhat in order to make the appeal of what he had to say even more dramatic than it already was. Except for one minor American official, all the individuals who met Brand in May and June 1944, Jewish, British, or American, were impressed by his honesty, his genuine sense of his mission, and his personal courage. There does not seem to be any contradiction between that impression and some other, less favorable character traits that emerge from a more detailed study of Brand's statements. His adventurousness, his addiction to drink, his tendency to seek an easy life, and his penchant for exaggeration—especially when it had to do with his own role—complement, rather than deny, the impression he made in 1944.

THE REACTIONS TO THE BRAND MISSION

What did Brand himself think of his mission? What did he suggest should be done by the Allied authorities? Did he think goods should be provided to the Nazis in return for Jewish lives?

Brand thought that one motivation for the Nazi offer might be the notion that "if they release the remaining two million Jews, they will be forgiven the extermination of six million Jews." He did not think, he told Shertok, that the Allies would give the Nazis 10,000 trucks, but the SS was utterly convinced that the Jews ruled the free world and that if they really wanted, they could send the trucks or indeed anything else.

According to Brand, however, he learned on the way to Istanbul and in Istanbul itself something about the second mission, namely that of Bandi Grosz. Grosz, he said, had hinted that it was his task to bring together Nazi and Allied representatives for talks that would go beyond the Jewish question. At first, Brand told Shertok:

I was convinced that were I to bring a positive answer (to the Germans), it would mean that I had brought salvation. Now that I have heard about Bandi's mission, I am no longer that sure. If I return with a negative answer, then immediate wholesale extermination will begin; possibly my family and my immediate friends will not be sent to the slaughterhouse straightaway, because they may want to keep an opening for further negotiations. Should I not return at all, all my friends will be murdered immediately . . . a slight chance exists that they may leave my family be in order to point to them and say: these are the family of the Jew Brand, whom we sent on a mission, and he ran away." [63]

Brand repeated the same ideas in Cairo. In essence, he said he should be permitted to return not with the idea of handing over trucks, but with the idea of perhaps offering money. The main thing, however, was the process of negotiation itself. As long as the Nazis thought the negotiations might lead to a result favorable to themselves, they would stop the murder. In short, he suggested negotiations with the ss. "The best thing I think would be that one, two, or three officers from Hungary should come to a neutral country, say Spain, or Turkey, or Switzerland, and English and American people, and myself too, and we should try to come to some sort of bargain." [64] As Hirschmann pointed out in his report on the interview with Brand, the Nazi idea about trucks was not very definite at all. "Brand's statement that the proposal connected with 10,000 lorries and other commodities was mentioned in an offhand way and in effect 'pulled out of the hat' by one of the German officers is a clear indication that this is not concrete or to be taken seriously." [65] Brand, then, thought that giving trucks was neither realistic nor important; negotiating about them was.

The reaction of the two Western Allies was one of consternation and some indecision, at least in the first stages. Laurence A. Steinhardt, U.S. ambassador in Ankara (and a Jew with very definite assimilationist and conservative tendencies), reported the essentials of the Brand mission to Washington on 25 May. [66] In Jerusalem, on 26 May, Shertok informed the High Commissioner of the same details; he himself had been informed by Venia Pomerantz on the previous day. As we have seen, MacMichael cabled the message to London immediately, adding Shertok's request that the gist of the message be brought to the attention of Weizmann in London and Nahum Goldman in New York.

Let us first examine the British reaction. The matter was considered serious enough to warrant a meeting of the War Cabinet Committee on the Reception and Accommodation of Refugees, which duly took place on 31 May. The proposals were judged by the participants at the meeting to be blackmail and a piece of political warfare. If the Germans had anything to propose, they could do so through the Protecting Power (Switzerland), and of course negotiations with the Gestapo were out of the question. So was the idea of handing over ten thousand lorries. The idea of an exit of Jews through Spain and Portugal was designed to embarrass Allied military operations (the Normandy landings were to take place exactly a week later). It was thought that the Germans might want to exchange Jews for German prisoners of war in Allied hands. This would leave the choice of the exchangees in Hitler's hands, and His Majesty's Government would lay themselves open to criticism if they did so. The Jewish Agency in Palestine was to be informed that there could be no negotiations with the Germans. And yet, the committee was facing a dilemma. In April 1943 the Anglo-American conference on refugees at Bermuda had reached no tangible results, and criticism of Britain's lack of action on the refugee problem was mounting. From all sides of the House of Commons, from the church dignitaries—especially the Archbishop of Canterbury—from many walks of life in wartime Britain, people were demanding that their government take some action about the persecutions of the Jews. The committee therefore decided that a "mere negative should not be opposed to any scheme which promises rescue of Jews," and that a communication in this sense be sent to the United States government. While it was thought that such a reaction might be welcomed by the Americans, the representative of the Foreign Office warned that the proposal, which actually deserved to be totally ignored if considered on its merits alone, might, God forbid, secure "sympathy . . . in Washington, where the President's War Refugee Board, backed by Mr. Morgenthau, had, partly for electoral reasons, committed itself to the 'rescue' of Jews." The opinion was expressed that "there seemed to be some danger that an indication that we might negotiate through a Protecting Power with the German Government might be followed up, and lead to an offer to unload an even greater number of Jews on to our hands." [67]

The points mentioned above were included in a memorandum sent to Washington on 5 June. On the negative side, the opposition to any kind of negotiations with the Germans was based on the general Anglo-American consensus of an unconditional German surrender. This had been fortified specifically for the whole problem of the refugees at the Bermuda conference, where any negotiations with Germany other than for the usual wartime exchanges of sick prisoners of war or civilians trapped by the war on the other side were agreed to be ruled out. On the positive side, however, the prospect was held out that numbers of Jews who might be "especially endangered" could be accommodated in Spain and Portugal. With all of European Jewry facing death, it was not made clear who the "especially endangered" Jews might be. No final answer should be given to the Nazis until an agreed Anglo-American stance was formulated, and the door should be kept open. That, in fact, was what the British suggested Shertok should tell his Zionist friends in Hungary.

One of the interesting points in analyzing the first responses is the fact that London was unaware of the Nazi declaration that the lorries would not be used against the West. Pomerantz did not transmit this information to Shertok, or Shertok did not volunteer it to MacMichael; in any case this obvious attempt to split the Allies was as yet unknown. Another point worth mentioning is that Grosz had been described in MacMichael's report as Brand's watchdog, and his role was simply ignored.

Foreign Secretary Eden disclosed the Brand mission to Weizmann on 5 June, and Weizmann's first reaction was that this was just a Nazi ploy to embarrass the Allies. At a second meeting on the following day, however, Weizmann changed his stance and demanded Shertok's immediate presence in London and a more positive attitude to the whole problem. Eden promised that His Majesty's Government would see to it that the door would be kept open—a phrase which was to recur in the correspondence during the following period.[68]

The British "fear" regarding U.S. policy had some basis in fact. On 22 January, Roosevelt set up the War Refugee Board, to be headed by the secretaries of State, War, and the Treasury. In fact, the acting director, John W. Pehle, formerly of the Treasury, was the guiding spirit; the full board met very rarely indeed. Pehle had sent out a cable to all United States missions abroad on 25 January, announcing that "action would be taken to forestall the plot of the Nazis to exterminate the Jews and other persecuted minorities in Europe."[69] The fact that the Jews were especially threatened and therefore had some claim to special attention was stated for the first time. Pehle was a non-Jew, and so were his Treasury colleagues who had impressed on their Jewish secretary, Henry Morgenthau, Jr., that drastic action was needed. The War Refugee Board was given rather unusual powers. It could issue licences to transfer funds into enemy territory, in practice in contravention to other war regulations; it could ask for and receive prior consideration for shipping of refugees, at a time when shipping was a major bottleneck in military operations; it was entitled to use State Department facilities both in Washington and at the different United States missions all over the globe. By implication, it could negotiate with the enemy over refugee matters, though it was understood that prior consent would be needed. What is more, the War Refugee Board used all these privileges in practice. It was the one clear instance during World War

II when moral and humanitarian considerations out-weighed and sometimes brushed aside considerations of utility and political or even strategic interests. This is of course not to say that the War Refugee Board was either free from faults, or did not encounter strong, often even bitter opposition from other elements in the wartime Washingtonian administrative labyrinth. Understandably enough, officials at State and at War saw the War Refugee Board as something of a nuisance, occasionally as a danger-ous menace. The Brand mission was just one of many issues where these tensions came to be expressed.

Edward R. Stettinius, the Acting Secretary of State, in-formed Nahum Goldman of the American branch of the Jewish Agency of the Brand affair on 7 June, as he had been asked to do in the British note. He told Goldman that the proposal would be seriously considered. Goldman suggested that a money ransom might be offered, and the money perhaps paid through Switzerland. Alternatively, the International Red Cross might be persuaded to look after the Jews, and receive payment for it. This of course was an idea that had been tried before, and was to be re-vived again before the war ended.[70]

In the War Refugee Board, Pehle had been busy. On 9 June, he could inform Edward Stettinius that Roosevelt had "agreed with our thought that we should keep the ne-gotiations open if possible," in order to gain time, "in the hope that meanwhile the lives of many intended victims will be spared."[71] On the same day, apparently with the President's explicit approval, Ira A. Hirschmann, a well-known Jewish businessman and supporter of the adminis-tration, was sent as War Refugee Board representative to Turkey to find out from Brand himself about his mission, and to report back to Washington. Hirschmann had been to Turkey for the War Refugee Board before, and could be relied upon to report back on the basis of his already considerable knowledge of the background. In its instructions to Steinhardt, the War Refugee Board, through Stettinius, took the same position as the British: not to close the door to further developments.[72]

The immediate problem for both governments was whether to inform the Soviets. Stettinius cabled Moscow on 9 June, asking Ambassador Averell Harriman to explain to the Soviets that the United States wanted to keep the door open, but instructing him to bring the facts to the attention of the Russians. A parallel message was sent to British Ambassador Sir Archibald Clark-Kerr. They informed Andrei Vyshinski, Deputy Soviet Foreign Minister, on 15 and 14 June, respectively, and Vyshinski replied to Harriman on the eighteenth. Harriman's cable reached Washington the twentieth.[73] The Soviet government, said Vyshinski, deemed it neither expedient nor permissible to negotiate with the German government regarding the problem mentioned in Harriman's note of the fifteenth. This attitude of the Soviet government could of course have been predicted. It is unclear whether the State Department and the White House turned to the Russians *because* they knew what the answer would be, or whether they turned to them *despite* this knowledge. In any case, any further meaningful *official* approaches to the Nazis related to the Brand mission were thereby effectively precluded. It was one thing to try to establish contacts designed to keep Jews alive while the contacts were maintained, and not to inform the Soviets about them officially; it was quite another thing altogether to establish such contacts after the Soviets had explicitly vetoed any such idea. In a sense, the American move and the Russian response meant the end of Brand's mission. In quite another, it meant that one phase of the affair had ended, but another one had only just begun. In any case, on 21 June, Steinhardt received a cable from Washington, in the wake of the Soviet reply, and was told not to do anything at all in the Brand affair, and to convey this information to Hirschmann. But Hirschmann no longer was in Turkey.

We have seen that Brand arrived in Syria on 7 June, and was interviewed by Shertok on the tenth. Hirschmann arrived in Turkey on the eleventh, and went on to Cairo, hoping to see Brand there. He interviewed him on the twenty-second, had several talks with Lord Moyne, the Resident Minister of State in the Middle East, and reported to Steinhardt and to Washington. Lord Moyne was worried lest the contacts with the Nazis be broken off and the Allies be accused of having caused the death of many innocent victims. He suggested that the Istanbul Agency group give some kind of an indication to the SS that its proposals were being studied. Hirschmann thought that this had best be left to Washington and London.[74] Shertok was flying to London (which he reached on the twenty-seventh), and no doubt decisions would be taken soon.

Pehle was dealing with the problem in conjunction and discussion with the State Department. It was not until 19 June that he informed Morgenthau, his real superior, for the first time regarding the Brand proposals. In the meantime, a reply had been worked out between him and State to the British note of 6 June. The American reply was delivered on the nineteenth, or one day before the devastating Soviet response was received. The American note ignored most of the reservations made by the British. It was based on a War Refugee Board draft of 13 June, and it indicated that the details of the Brand proposals were not as important as the possibility that the process of negotiations itself might lead to the saving of lives, because if the process were dragged out, the war might end in the meantime. It was, the Americans said, agreed that large numbers of Jewish refugees escaping from Nazi areas might prejudice military operations and that such a movement was therefore not practical. But, they said, the Germans should be made aware that the two governments would be prepared to consider temporary havens for "all Jews and similar persons in imminent danger of death." [75]

The British agonized over their reply for almost two weeks. On 26 June, Eden signed a Foreign Office memorandum which stuck to the idea that the Brand proposals be kept in play in order to avoid the accusation of indifference "to the whole Jewish catastrophe." [76] The Germans should be told that the Allies were willing to accept certain groups of Jews about whom negotiations through the Swiss had been proceeding for some time: a group of Rabbis, for Mauritius; 5,000 women and children from the Balkans to Palestine; and so on. Spain and Portugal should be invited to offer hospitality, at British and American expense, to a "stated number" of Jews, but not to "all" Jews, as the Americans had suggested. Brand should be released, and tell the Germans that they would be approached through the Swiss. The interesting thing is that the British knew of the Soviet refusal to allow the Allies to negotiate. But they still wanted to keep the doors open. They therefore proposed to negotiate quite officially through the Swiss, and wanted to instruct Brand and Shertok that no ransom would be paid, and no direct negotiations would take place. On the whole, however, Eden did not want to be bothered with the whole problem. On 28 June, Weizmann and Shertok asked to see him to discuss the Brand mission. Eden minuted: "Must I? Which of my colleagues looks after this? Minister of State (Richard Law) or Mr. (George) Hall? At least one of them responsible should be there if I have to see these two Jews. Weizmann doesn't usually take much time." [77]

In the end, Hall saw "these two Jews" on 30 June. They suggested that the Germans be told through the Swiss of Allied readiness to meet with them to discuss the rescue of Jews in general. The War Refugee Board should meet with representatives of the Gestapo, provided deportations were stopped. Radio warnings should be issued to Hungarian railwaymen not to carry Jews to death camps. Finally, they demanded that the death camps at Auschwitz be bombed.[78]

Two comments are in order on these new proposals. First, detailed reports regarding the Auschwitz death camp and the gassing installations in it were received in Slovakia from two Slovak Jews who escaped from the camp on 7 April 1944. These testimonies, and those of two other Jews who escaped from Auschwitz on 27 May, were carefully written down by members of the Slovak "working group," and transmitted to the Vatican, to Switzerland, and to Hungary. It is not quite clear why these reports did not reach Jewish organizations in Switzerland until about 21 June, but when they did, these groups immediately informed the British and American representatives. The British Foreign Office learned of the report from a cable which the Jewish Agency representative at Geneva, Richard Lichtheim, sent to his organization in London through the British mission at Berne on 26 June. After that date, similar cables based on these reports started coming in, the Czechoslovak government also transmitted the report, and early in July the report itself came in, from Stockholm, and then again from the Czech government in London.[79] There was therefore no reason to disregard the appeals for help from the Jewish Agency. Indeed, notes by Foreign Office officials on the report from Sweden about the Auschwitz gas chambers no longer expressed disbelief. Faced with the Nazi policy, they said, "it is difficult to see what can be done by those who like ourselves would do everything in our power to stop it."[80]

Second, the idea of bombing either the death camps or the railways leading up to them, or both, had been broached on 2 June by two seemingly different sources: by Itzhak Gruenbaum, the chairman of the Jewish Agency Rescue Committee in Jerusalem, in a cable transmitted to Washington by consul Pinkerton in Palestine; and by Isaac Sternbuch, Swiss representative of the Va'ad Hahatzalah (Rescue Committee) of the Orthodox Rabbis in the United States, in a cable transmitted by the American delegate at Berne.[81] The idea was then repeated a number of times on different occasions throughout June, with Gruenbaum again repeating it to London on 29 June.[82] On all these occasions, the proposal can be traced back to a message sent by Rabbi Weissmandel about the middle of May, which reached Istanbul before Brand left for Syria.[83] The same message also forms the basis of a cable from Roswell D. McClelland, War Refugee Board representative at Berne, to Washington, on 24 June.[84] It seems strange that the very sensible idea of using Allied military power to prevent the murder of Hungarian Jews should have occurred first to an ultra-Orthodox Slovak rabbi, but that is a fact. It is even stranger that the idea was not acted upon by the military men of both Western powers.

The reports on gassings at Auschwitz did not much change Foreign Office attitudes. The Jewish Agency submitted yet another aide-memoire on 6 July. By that time, a month had passed since the arrival of Brand on the Syrian border. In the meantime, the Agency paper screamed, four hundred thousand Jews had been sent to the death camps, and what went on there was known. The "stage of temporizing, in the hope of prolonging the victims' lives, is over." Negotiations were essential. A War Refugee Board and a British representative should meet the Nazis. Brand, and Grosz if possible, should return. The Nazis might let out some Jews. It might "boil down to a question of money, and we believe that the ransom should be paid." The Allies should publish a declaration that they would admit refugees released by the Nazis. Another warning should be sent to the Hungarians, in which Stalin should be asked to join. The camps and the railways should be bombed.

Faced with this paper, Ian L. Henderson, a high Foreign Office official, decided to warn Eden of a "complete surrender to Jewish pressure irrespective of whether political results may follow." Referring to the main point, namely that of the negotiations, Alec Randall of the Foreign Office commented, "We can't have this, and the U.S. government having now agreed not to negotiate with the Germans except with Soviet agreement, must realize that these Jewish proposals for a meeting are impossible." [85] The British were acting out of an understanding—or misunderstanding—that "the U.S. government, particularly in [an] election year, is desperately anxious to show that nothing, however fantastic, has been neglected that might lead to the rescue of Jews." Had it not been for what the British thought they had to do to accommodate American sensitivities, they would not have hesitated to "dismiss the Gestapo proposals with contempt" right at the outset. [86]

In line with this basic British approach, a cable was sent to the British embassy in Washington that was to represent the furthest limit to which the British government was prepared to commit itself. Sent on 1 July, the cable analyzed the Brand proposals as designed to produce a split between the Russians and their western Allies; furthermore, they were intended "to elicit a rejection, which would then be represented as justification for extreme measures against Jews" (one wonders what more extreme measures could have been taken beyond total murder). They should really have been rejected, but they had been "kept in play in the hope of staving off disaster." Therefore, the British again proposed to send Brand back, and negotiate through the Swiss, mainly for the release of children. Spain should also be approached to receive "manageable numbers of Jewish refugees." In Shertok's words, "a 'carrot' should be dangled before the Germans in the shape of agreement by the U.K. and U.S. to discuss with them the question of Jewish rescue." Finally, the British note asked the ambassador to find out whether Shertok was correct in stating that the War Refugee Board was permitted to contact the Germans directly. The British thought in any case that any step to be taken would have to receive prior Soviet approval.[87]

The British attitude was undoubtedly influenced by two brief interventions of Churchill. Although motivated by the same deep feeling for the Jewish victims, and by a deep hatred for the Nazis and all their works, they tended to operate in two contradictory ways. The first one was in a brief minute Churchill wrote on 29 June, after reading Lichtheim's report on the gassings at Auschwitz. It said: "Foreign Secretary. What can be done? What can be said?" It was this minute that undoubtedly influenced the more positive Foreign Office attitude at the end of June and the first days of July. When Eden then brought the results of the deliberations at the Foreign Office to Churchill's attention, and included in his report the ideas of approaching the Swiss to rescue children and investigate the possibility of bombing Auschwitz, Churchill replied on 7 July: "You and I are in entire agreement. Get anything out of the Air Force you can and invoke me if necessary. Certainly appeal to Stalin. On no account have the slightest negotiations, direct or indirect, with the Huns."[88]

Action was taken by Eden on Churchill's remark regarding the bombing of Auschwitz—but the Air Ministry, under Sir Archibald Sinclair, replied that the bombing was technically impossible. On the other hand, his directive not to have anything to do, directly or indirectly, with the Germans was interpreted by Eden as a refusal to negotiate through the Protecting Power. Thus, on 13 July, at a meeting of the Cabinet Committee, Eden declared that the policy had changed: no approach through the Swiss was now contemplated.[89]

As if the new British attitude were not enough to bury the Brand mission, the Americans now insisted on telling the Soviets what they had not known on 9 June, when Harriman was first told to inform the Soviets of the Brand proposals: that the Nazis had "promised" not to use the trucks in the West, but only against the Russians. On 7 July, instructions were sent by the State Department to tell the Soviets all the details. The British had attempted to dissuade the Americans from thus finally dismissing all possibility to act upon the Nazi offer. The Americans were at that time trying to keep in the Soviets' good graces, and must have feared that if, as was inevitable in the end, the Soviets should discover the full details of the offer themselves, the damage would be much greater. They therefore explicitly overrode the British objections and Harriman was instructed to tell the Russians.[90] Brand and Grosz could not return without Soviet agreement.

The contortions of Anglo-American policies regarding the Nazi offer received a new and somewhat unexpected turn during the second week of July 1944. The British Cabinet Committee met on 13 July. Eden declared there that up until now the object of British policy had been to spin out the negotiations in the hope of saving lives. Now the Prime Minister had indicated that negotiations through the Swiss were to be avoided. Not only could there now be no negotiations at all, but the sinister motives behind the Nazi proposals had become much clearer: "Mr. Randall (Foreign Office) informed the Committee that a report had just been received showing that the approach by Brand and Grosz had been intended as cover for a separate peace intrigue. It was stated that high Gestapo officials were implicated, their object being to put forward vague hints of peace proposals which might embarrass us with the U.S.S.R." The whole business was a trap, Eden concluded. A message from the Prime Minister to the President might be needed to explain the British change of policy. This might also produce publication of the offer by the Germans or the Jews [*sic*], in which case a full exposition of the facts would be necessary.[91]

On 18 July, accordingly, a cable was sent via the British ambassador in Washington to the State Department, explaining the change of British policy. Until now, the note said, the British had thought that the proposals should be investigated and Brand retained in the hope that a serious proposal might emerge or that, in the interval, the murder of the Jews would cease. Neither had occurred. On the other hand, a most dangerous development had come about: "we now have evidence that the Brand mission was intended as cover for an approach to us or to the Americans on the question of a separate peace, not seriously intended, no doubt, except in an attempt to prejudice our relations with the Soviet Government." The Gestapo agent (Grosz) should be retained; if Brand still wished to return to Hungary, he could do so, provided the security people had no objections, but he must be told that the Allies "cannot be expected to take any cognisance of the suggestions he brought or the channels through which they were conveyed."[92]

What was the evidence?

THE MISSION OF BANDI GROSZ

Bandi Grosz, it will be remembered, left for Syria from Istanbul on 1 June. He was arrested and brought to Cairo. There he was interrogated from 6 June to 22 June by the

Mideast Intelligence Service. The interview was written up and ready for distribution on 4 July, and it must have reached the Foreign Office about a week later,[93] which would explain the change in British policy on the thirteenth.

After the arrest of the Abwehr people on 7 May, the SD in Budapest—Klages, Laufer, and Klausnitzer—must have decided that Grosz was their man to transmit a message to Istanbul. According to Grosz, he met the group on 13 May, and Klages explained to him that they had reported Brand's readiness to go and get war material in exchange for Jews to Berlin and had received instructions that Brand must be sent on his mission. The Jews would be sent (to Palestine, Klages said) and thus burden the British with vast problems. The next day (14 May), however, after the background of the Brand mission had been explained to Grosz—or at least that part of it destined for his ears—Klages talked to Grosz about the stalemate in the war, which necessitated a breakthrough. The time had come for the war between Germany and the Western Allies to cease, and a united front against Russia had become necessary. Was it possible to negotiate with the Allies through the Zionists? Grosz said that this might be a possibility.

Klages now asked Grosz "whether he knew of any way to arrange a meeting in any neutral country between two or three high SD officers and two or three high British and American officers for the purpose of opening negotiations on the subject of a separate peace between the SD and the Allies (excluding Russia)." Grosz thought he could do that more easily than Brand could get his lorries, but asked "why he, a petty smuggler, should be chosen to do this instead of, for instance, Herr von Papen, Germany's diplomatic representative in Turkey." Klages said he did not want to negotiate with diplomats, but with military representatives. Anyway, he said, the SD was "having trouble

with the [Nazi] Foreign Office," and that was the real
reason for Brand's mission:

If Brand was successful in delivering war material, or at least a
large amount of money to Germany, the Foreign Office could
not turn around to the SD and ask why they were negotiating
with the Zionists, and why they had altered their policy concerning the Jews. Brand's mission was really only a sop to the
Foreign Office, and camouflage for the mission with which the
SD was contemplating sending Grosz, namely to arrange a meeting between the SD and the British and Americans . . . the SD
was now the real directing power in Germany, and whatever
'Heinrich mit (dem) Augenglass' [Heinrich with the spectacles],
Himmler, decreed, had to be carried out. The SD was genuinely
keen to negotiate a separate peace and to obtain its own 'security.' "[94]

Grosz was to arrange for such a meeting between the SD
and the Allies through the Zionists. If this proved impossible, he was to use his contacts with the American Intelligence officer Schwarz to arrange for the meeting. The
Allies could meet with any SD officer except for Himmler,
who could not leave Europe. If Grosz and Brand returned
to Hungary without having accomplished anything at all,
they were to make another attempt through Switzerland,
with the representative there of the American Jewish Joint
Distribution Committee (JDC), the main American Jewish
rescue and welfare agency.[95] If that failed, they should try
again through Dr. Joseph J. Schwartz, the JDC's European
director, who was working out of Lisbon. Grosz was to return by 29 May.

   In analyzing Grosz's testimony, one must realize that
this took place two months before the attempt on Hitler's
life on 20 July. We know already that the Abwehr and
Schellenberg's SD shared the opinion that Germany was
losing the war. We also know that Himmler was aware of
the opposition groups who were planning action against
Hitler, though he probably did not know that Klaus von

Stauffenberg was planning to assassinate the Führer. A peace feeler parallel to the Brand-Grosz mission was put out through Stockholm at the same time. Iver Olsen, the War Refugee Board representative at Stockholm, reported on 28 June that an ss man by the name of Peter Bruno Kleist had offered the release of two thousand Latvian Jews for $2 million, or, later, two million Swedish kroner.[96] It soon became clear that this was another gauche attempt to contact American diplomatic representatives, with an ultimate aim that went far beyond the fates of two thousand Latvian Jews—or, later, 100,000 Estonians. Such feelers could not have been put out without Himmler's express approval. What Grosz reported in Klages's name in this connection sounds genuine enough. The very turn of the phrase *"Heinrich mit (dem) Augenglass"* was current only among the ss. Grosz would not have been aware of it, unless it had been mentioned by an ss man in his presence.

Why had Grosz, an unsavory character and a known and lowly agent, been chosen for such a top secret and important mission? Part of the answer, it seems, was provided by Grosz himself. There was a bitter enmity between the ss and the Nazi Foreign Office. A German could not be sent abroad, because then the Ribbentrop people would have asked awkward questions that might be reported to the Führer—and Himmler stood in fear and awe before the man whom he wanted to succeed or even supersede.[97] On the other hand, somebody had to be sent who already had contacts with Allied services. There was only one such person in the Third Reich, and he was sitting right in Budapest under the SD's nose: Andor "Bandi" Grosz.

The contacts were to be established between the Allies and the "SD," i.e., the ss representatives, not official German negotiators. Obviously, given Himmler's intrigue against Ribbentrop and his desire to make a separate peace, this was the only way the thing could be engineered. If Ribbentrop and Hitler got wind of Grosz's mission and any subsequent meetings, Himmler would be in a very awkward spot indeed. If, however, Grosz was covered by the Brand mission, which was a patriotic attempt to get war materials for the hard-pressed Thousand-Year Reich in exchange for Jews who were doomed to death anyway, then Himmler had a good excuse in any eventuality. The very fact that Grosz was a worthless lout could be utilized in an emergency: whose word should the Führer believe if the affair blew up, that of a Jewish criminal or that of his faithful and obedient Heinrich?

The conclusion is inevitable that Eichmann received his orders to add Grosz to the mission ultimately from Himmler; that from the moment this happened, Grosz's mission to prepare the ground for a separate peace became the main purpose of the journey to Istanbul. If Brand succeeded in getting war materials, or money, or starting negotiations that would lead to the same result as sought by the Grosz mission, so much the better. In any case, under the cover of the fantastic proposals brought by Brand, Grosz would be able to contact the Allied Intelligence Services, which would of course immediately recognize the importance of what he had to say. His mission was the main message to the Allies. Brand's mission was an adjunct affair at best, at worst a smoke screen. The purpose, ultimately, of both was the same: a separate peace with the West and an alliance against Russia.

The Western Allies did indeed recognize the importance of the Grosz mission, though it took them some time, due to the secretiveness of their own Intelligence Services and quite probably because of sheer inefficiency. Of course, from the Allied point of view, this was an outrageous, stupid, and impossible suggestion. If the release of Jews was connected with negotiations with the ss on such a basis, then nothing could or should be done.

It is not quite clear whether the British transmitted to the Americans the full protocol of the Grosz interrogation. In any case, the Americans, while agreeing not to pursue the actual Brand offer any further, were now aware of the fact that some possibility existed of saving Jews by negotiation. This was to have crucial importance in the next few weeks.

Was the Jewish Agency, and especially Shertok, aware of the Nazi peace feelers? Clearly, yes. Shertok was told by Brand of Grosz's mission in Aleppo, and Brand explained that he had had the first inkling of it on the plane, and then had received a more detailed account from Grosz in Istanbul. From the context it appears that Brand did not doubt Grosz's word: the feelers were genuine.

In the aftermath and the publicity of the Brand mission, the crucial part played by Grosz was quickly forgotten. Postwar discussion hardly ever mentioned Grosz. The "trucks for blood" proposal captured the imagination, and the historical picture was thus completely distorted. In 1954, at the "Kastner trial," Grosz made one more appearance, before disappearing into a well-deserved oblivion. He was asked to testify against Kastner by Shmuel Tamir, because an association between a person of Grosz's character and Kastner fitted into the brief that Tamir had prepared, which included accusations against the Jewish Agency's representative, Kastner, of having collaborated with the Nazis. He even argued that the Agency had failed to prosecute Grosz as a traitor after the war because it had been afraid of what Grosz might say regarding its own collaboration with Germany. Grosz, at the trial, cut through this vicious nonsense by simply telling his story. Not only Tamir, but the prosecuting counsel, Haim

Cohen (defending Kastner), as well, argued, explicitly or by implication, that Grosz was a liar and a dirty little smuggler (Cohen called him *"Gauner,"* a lout), and that his whole story about a separate peace was his own invention. In short, Grosz's story did not fit in with either side at that historic trial. The truth was too simple for the complicated constructions of postwar Jewish politicians and pleaders of special causes who were trying to accuse or defend the people who, under the Nazi threat of death, negotiated with the Devil for the lives of Jews.[98] Yet the unbelievable, the impossible, was the truth: the SS wanted a separate peace, without Hitler's knowledge, and they had chosen Bandi Grosz to try to establish the first contacts. The sale of Jews might be a first step in such negotiations, and in any case, as the Jews were the controlling factor in the Allied world in Nazi eyes, the way to the Allied governments had to lead through the Jewish representatives in the free world.

THE AFTERMATH

The British government, worried and perturbed by the Grosz disclosure, did not wait very long before deciding to deal a final death blow to the Brand-Grosz affair. Already in its cable to Washington of 18 July it had hinted that if the situation became unpleasant, it would publish the whole affair and thus make any future negotiations impossible, and at the same time give the Russians the definitive assurance that no contacts with the Germans were taking place behind their backs. The Foreign Office, no doubt at Eden's instigation, leaked the Brand-Grosz proposals to the press. On 19 July, the *New York Herald Tribune* exposed the whole story under a London by-line dated 18 July, the day the cable was sent to the State Department. Termed the most monstrous blackmail attempt in history, the offer was described as intended to place the Allies before the choice of either prolonging the war by accepting large numbers of refugees in return for supplying the Nazis with essential war materials, or "accepting responsibility for the fate of hundreds of thousands of Jews" by refusing the offer. The next day the *London Times* appeared with the headline "A Monstrous Offer." "A short time ago a prominent Hungarian Jew and a German official, whose job obviously was to control his actions and movements, arrived in Turkey, and managed to get a message" to British officials containing the Nazi offer. The *Times* also mentioned the statement that the trucks would not be used against the West, and stated that the coarse attempt to split the Allied front would fail miserably. Similar headlines and stories were carried on the same day by the *Manchester Guardian* and other British dailies. The contents of these articles were duly broadcast by the BBC. On 21 July, no less a man that Wickham Steed, the journalist, broadcast over the Eastern Service of the BBC that "a rich industrialist, a Hungarian Jew, accompanied by two German officials, [came] to Turkey to negotiate with the British the eventual migration of the remaining 400,000 Jews still alive in Hungary," etc. "It is needless to say that this humanitarian blackmail was not accepted by the British who informed the U.S. and Soviet Governments of the German proposal." [99] The British certainly made sure that nothing should come of the Brand mission.

Eyebrows were naturally raised in Berlin, and we have some evidence of the trouble that Himmler got into through the publication of the Brand proposals. But the Himmler plan justified itself: he could now point to the fact that he was trying to get important war materials from the Allies, and there surely was nothing wrong with that. If, in fact, our analysis of Himmler's motives is correct, we should expect that even after the obvious failure of the Brand-Grosz mission, the Nazis would continue to try to establish contact with the West. This, indeed, is what happened, and not only on the part of the Nazis, but on the Jewish Agency side as well. Both parties, for opposing reasons, wanted negotiations of some kind to take place. Shertok in London thought that the Intergovernmental Committee on Refugees (IGC), a body resurrected from the dead by the abortive Bermuda conference in April 1943, should be the agency through which negotiations should take place. The IGC included neutral members, and its vice-director, the Swiss Kullmann, should go to Budapest and talk to the Nazis. But the British demurred—the IGC was a body of Allied as well as neutral countries, and a representative of such an organization could not possibly negotiate with the enemy.[100] Desperate at the attitude of the British, the Agency tried to influence the Americans. "The Jewish Agency earnestly appeals to you," cabled Ben Gurion to Roosevelt via Nahum Goldman, "not to allow this unique and possibly last chance of saving the remains of European Jewry to be lost, although it is fully realized that the exigencies of war are [a] primary consideration." He asked that "suitable arrangements be made to discuss the [Brand] proposal with representatives of the enemy group."[101]

When Brand and Grosz failed to return, pressure was exercised by Eichmann on Kastner and the Va'adah in Budapest. Hansi Brand and Kastner cabled on 20 June that the journey of "the two" had only been preparatory. The Nazis thought that now Schröder (Laufer's alias) should meet with Schwarz (the American Intelligence agent in Istanbul). On 23 June, a somewhat garbled message by Kastner in fact invited Bader, who in Pomerantz's absence had sent the reply cables to Budapest, to come and meet the Nazis in Hungary. In his letter to Pomerantz the next day, Bader agreed that this should be done.[102] The cable was repeated, this time explicitly, about 2 July. Eliezer Kaplan, Jewish Agency treasurer, who happened to be in Istanbul at the time, told Bader that he could not go without British approval. The request of the Agency to send Bader to Hungary was transmitted to the Foreign Office on 5 July. Weizmann and Shertok raised it again with Eden the next day, and Eden asked for advice from his officials. The advice was, of course, to reject this new suggestion. Bader was a Palestinian, that is, a British citizen, and no negotiation between a British and a German citizen was permissible. Besides, Eden was to beware of the Agency's machinations. They might make "contacts behind our back" with the Germans over the rescue of Jews, and this was a danger. In the meantime, on 8 July, German pressure on Bader to go increased. Colonel Stiller of the German consulate in Istanbul asked for an interview with Bader, which took place in a public library. Stiller offered to fly Bader to Berlin [!] straightaway. Bader had to reply that without Allied permission he could not go. Barlas cabled to Shertok, but in the meantime the British decision was being formulated. Shertok heard of it on the thirteenth, and cabled to Goldman accordingly. On the fifteenth, he received the official refusal of the Foreign Office. But, as U.S. ambassador to London Winant commented rightly: the offer to Bader indicated German seriousness in seeking these contacts. One might add that the invitation to Berlin probably meant that at least Schellenberg would have received the Istanbul emissary.[103]

Once the Bader trip fell through, the Germans, apparently at the suggestion of Kastner, tried to get American approval to negotiate with Schwartz of the JDC, Lisbon. The suggestion reached Pehle of the War Refugee Board on 26 July, and he rejected it, in agreement with Stettinius, the next day.[104] The reason was slightly, but significantly, different. No ulterior motives were imputed to the Jews in general or to the JDC in particular, but Schwartz was an American citizen. If, however, someone could be found that was not an Allied citizen, could he negotiate with the Nazis? The British attitude was no. The War Refugee Board's attitude had not changed, despite Grosz. We cannot afford to slam the door to negotiations, said John W. Pehle.[105] In the latter part of July, that remained War Refugee Board policy. In the last days of July and early in August, the idea crystallized of nominating Saly Mayer, Swiss representative of the JDC, to negotiate with the Nazis. These negotiations started on 21 August, but they did not belong to the Brand-Grosz affair, and they have been described elsewhere.[106]

There was no British veto on Brand himself. The British had no reason to keep him, and they offered the Agency to take him, after some procrastination. They even agreed that he should return to Hungary. The Agency was offered the choice between that and a release to Palestine. Brand was not told of that choice. The Agency decided to take him to Palestine, and not to send him to certain, and futile, death in Budapest. He would have returned with empty hands. He became a bitter enemy both of the British and of the Agency itself. He never really understood what had happened to him. Grosz stayed, quite happily, in British detention until the end of the war. The mission had failed.

CONCLUSIONS

Who had sent Brand and Grosz, and why? They had been sent by the SS, on Himmler's orders, to pave the way for a separate peace. The Brand proposal was both an opening gambit in any such negotiations, and also a cover for the real mission. The Jews were Himmler's hostages.

Their fellow Jews were, in Nazi eyes, in control of the West. They would therefore be interested in a process of talks that might save their relatives and friends—for a consideration. Did the ss really believe the war materials could be obtained? Probably yes, as part of the process of negotiations and as one of its results. Were they willing to release Jews against such materials and in the process of talks regarding peace feelers? Yes, most probably. They knew that the war was lost and the hoped-for talks, as well as possible materials, were more important to them than the Jews, whether alive or dead. The very same inhuman attitude that caused them to be able to murder masses of Jewish people, also enabled them to trade Jews for any-thing—trucks, soap, or peace feelers. There even was an ideological justification for this: if the Jews were spread all over the world, or even if they were concentrated in one place, they would arouse enmity and antisemitism, which would aid Nazi Germany.

Was there any real possibility of the Allies accepting the proposals as they stood? Hardly. But that is not really the point. The Allies were not required to hand over war materials, interfere with the prosecution of the war, or talk peace with the Nazis. All they need have done, as Shertok and Brand both told them, was to negotiate. The process of negotiation itself, without leading to any con-crete result, might have saved lives. This is exactly what Saly Mayer did in his talks with the ss, which lasted from August 1944 to February 1945. It is impossible to say how many lives, if any, would have been saved. The moral imperative, however, of trying to save even one life was ignored by an Allied world that by its lack of action de-nied the rationale of its war against the absolute evil that was Nazism. The moral imperative was not anachronistic. It was stated by the Jewish representatives, by Weizmann, Ben Gurion, Shertok, and others. It was weighed in the

balance of war policies of the Western Allies. It was completely ignored by the Soviets. In the West, where it was
weighed, it was rejected. The real conclusion is that Brand
did not fail. It was the West that failed.

Notes

CHAPTER I

1. *World Jewish Congress Bulletin* (London, Jan. 1940).
2. Hermann Rauschning, *Gesprache mit Hitler* (Vienna, 1973), p. 223 (my translation).
3. Uriel Tal, "Forms of Pseudo-Religion in the German Kultur-bereich Prior to the Holocaust," *Immanuel*, no. 3 (Jerusalem, 1974): 68–73.
4. Adolf Hitler, *Mein Kampf*, trans. James Murphy (London: Hurst and Blackett, 1962), p. 261. Cf. also Rauschning, *Gesprache mit Hitler*, p. 222.
5. "This caste must be totally exterminated"—Jakob Fries, *Ueber die Gefährdung des Wohlstandes der Deutschen durch die Juden* (Heidelberg, 1816), p. 18.
6. Rauschning, *Gesprache mit Hitler*, p. 223.
7. Norbert Masur, *En Jude talar med Himmler* (Stockholm, 1945).
8. "Der Jude ist kein Mensch; er ist eine Fäulniserscheinung"—quoted in Krausnick, "Judenverfolgungen," in Helmut Krausnick et al., *Anatomy of the SS-State* (London: Paladin, 1970), p. 309, footnote 16.
9. Nuremberg Document PS-3358, 25 January 1939; for the Schacht-Rublee negotiations, see Yehuda Bauer, *My Brother's Keeper: A History of the American Jewish Joint Distribution, 1929–1939* (Philadelphia: Jewish Publication Society, 1974), pp. 274–85.
10. See Leni Yahil, "Madagascar—Hazon Ta'atu'im shel Pitron Ha-she'elah Hayehudit," in *Yalkut Moreshet*, no. 19 (June 1975): 159–74.
11. *Vierteljahreshefte fur Zeitgeschichte*, 5 Jg., Heft 2 (April 1957): 196–98.
12. Dr. Franz W. Stahlecker (Einsatzgruppe A), Dr. Otto Rasch (Einsatzgruppe C), Dr. Otto Ohlendorf (Einsatzgruppe D).
13. The account of the destruction process is largely based on Kraus-

nick, "Judenverfolgungen"; Raul Hilberg, *The Destruction of the European Jews* (Chicago: Quadrangle, 1961); Shmuel Krakowski, *Halehima Hayehudit Bepolin* (Jerusalem, 1977); and Yisrael Gutnam, *Yehudei Warsha* (Jerusalem, 1977).

14. See Yehuda Bauer, "When Did They Know?," in *Midstream*, April 1968, p. 51; Ernest Hearst, "The British and the Slaughter of the Jews," part 1, in *Wiener Library Bulletin*, vol. 21, no. 1 (Winter 1966/7).

15. "Life in the Polish Ghetto," *Jewish Frontier*, May 1942, p. 13; a summary of the Polish notes will be found in the *Polish Fortnightly Review*, 15 July 1942; material on the Baltic murders, in the *London Evening Standard*, 16 June 1942, among others.

16. *The Ghetto Speaks* (New York), no. 1, 1 August 1942.

17. Arthur D. Morse, *While Six Million Died: A Chronicle of American Apathy* (New York: Random House, 1967), p. 8. Riegner's cable originated from two sources, one a German businessman, and one a famous German economist, Artur Sommer. Sommer had become a German army liaison officer to the counterespionage (Abwehr) of Admiral Canaris. He was also a member of the German delegation to the Swiss-German economic negotiations in 1942. The information regarding Hitler's plans he left with a Jewish savant in Switzerland, Edgar Salin, who then gave it to Chaim Pozner of the Jewish Agency office in Geneva on the one hand, and an American businessman on the other hand. Pozner gave it to Benjamin Segalowitz, a well-known Swiss Jewish journalist, who in turn handed it to Riegner on 1 August. Riegner verified and checked it for a week before handing it over to the American and British embassies, who in the meantime must have received it from two other sources (the American businessman, and Pozner, who was also connected to the British embassy).

18. Morse, *While Six Million Died*, pp. 8–22.

19. P. C. Squire on his conversation with C. J. Burckhardt in Geneva Files of World Jewish Congress, 7 November 1942. I am indebted to Dr. Riegner for permission to use these files.

20. Sikorski Institute, London: Sprawozdanie, 5 August 1942: "Jesli sprawozdanie polskie z kraju nie znajdują u narodów anglosaskich w pelni wiary jako wiecz neiprawdopodobne, to przeciez powinny dotrzec do rządow ich sprawozdanie żydowskie."

21. Note by Edward Raczysnki, Polish ambassador, to Anthony Eden, 9 December 1942, Public Record Office, London, document FP688-29-ERD/7147.

22. *The Ghetto Speaks*, no. 16, 1 October 1943.

23. Moreshet Archive (hereafter cited as MA), D.1.698. Bader did not only write to his chiefs in Palestine. On 20 January 1943 he submitted a memorandum to the Papal Nuncio in Istanbul, Agnelo G. Roncalli (later to become John XXIII), which Roncalli promised to

send to Pius XII, in which he reported the massacres in a most immediate and direct way: "The situation of the Jews in the occupied countries is a terrible one. The numbers of the massacred reach millions. It is impossible to repeat the details regarding the massacre of defenseless people—aged, sick, women, children—without crying or freezing into terrorized immobility" (Man kann nicht die Einzelheiten dieser Massakrierung von Wehrlosen—Greisen, Kranken, Frauen, Kindern—widerholen ohne zu weinen oder vor Entsetzen zu erstarren.")

24. Bader to Palestine, 23 October 1943, MA-D.1.705.

25. Bader to Bornstein, 9 March 1943, MA-D.1.730. Peake in Hansard, Commons, 19 May 1943, colls. 1,117–1,204. On 28 May, Paul Baerwald of the American Jewish Joint Distribution Committee (JDC) wrote a letter to Sumner Welles at the State Department, in which he offered JDC's help in any practical steps the government might wish to take, directly or as a member of the Intergovernmental Committee for Refugees, looking toward the rescue or the relief of distressed Jews in Axis-occupied territories (JDC file "Administration-U.S. State Department, 1939–1945"). There was no problem: there were no plans for any steps. JDC itself was also involved—just like all the other major agencies—in postwar planning.

26. Lichtheim to Bader, 12 April 1943, MA-D.1.814.

27. MA-D.1.913.

28. *Zionist Review,* 22 September 1944.

CHAPTER 2

1. A. M. MacDonald, ed., *Chambers Twentieth Century Dictionary* (Totowa, N.J.: Littlefield, 1975).

2. Emil L. Fackenheim, "The Nazi Holocaust as a Persisting Trauma for the Non-Jewish Mind," *Journal of the History of Ideas* 36, no. 2 (April–May 1975): 369–76; idem, "Concerning Authentic and Unauthentic Responses to the Holocaust," lecture at "The Holocaust—A Generation After" conference, New York, March 1975 (to be published shortly).

3. Cf. Jacob Robinson's section on the Holocaust in *Encyclopaedia Judaica* (Jerusalem, 1971); cf. also Keter Publishing House Staff, *Holocaust* (Jerusalem: Israel Pocket Library, 1974), pp. 52–55. Of all the attempts to calculate the losses of the Jewish people in the Holocaust era, Robinson's seems to be the most authoritative (cf. George Wellers, "La Mythomanie Nazie," *Le Monde Juif,* no. 86 [April–June 1977]).

4. "Teaching the Holocaust," *New York Times,* 9 November 1977; letter from Paul Ronald, *New York Times,* 15 October 1977.

5. Gerd Korman, "The Holocaust in American Historical Writing," *Societas* 2 (summer, 1972):251–70.

6. A. Roy Eckardt, "Is the Holocaust Unique," *Worldview*, Sept. 1974, pp. 21–35.

7. See, for instance, Uriel Tal, "On the Structure of Political Theology and Myth in Germany Prior to the Holocaust," lecture at "The Holocaust—A Generation After" conference, New York, March 1975.

8. Alex Bein, "The Jewish Parasite," in Leo Baeck Institute of Jews from Germany, *Leo Baeck Yearbook*, vol. 9 (London, 1964), pp. 3–39.

9. Norman Cohn, *Warrant for Genocide* (London: Eyre & Spottiswood, 1967).

10. See Elie Wiesel, "Talking and Writing and Keeping Silent," in *The German Church Struggle and the Holocaust,* ed. Franklin H. Littell and Hubert G. Locke (Detroit: Wayne State University Press, 1974), p. 272.

11. Cf. for instance Mark Arnold-Foster, *The World at War* (London: Collins, 1973), p. 293.

12. On the so-called "AB-Aktion" against the Polish intelligentsia and other such actions, see Martin Broszat, *Nationalsozialistische Polenpolitik* (Stuttgart, 1961), pp. 38–48, 182–87.

13. Reimund Schnabel, *Macht ohne Moral* (Frankfurt, 1957), p. 404.

14. Raphael Lemkin, *Axis Rule in Occupied Europe* (1943; reprint ed., New York: Howard Fertig, 1973), pp. xi–xii.

15. I. Caban and Z. Mańkowski, *Związek Walki Zbrojnej i Armia Krajowa w Okręgu Lubelskim,* 1939–1944, tom II, Dokumenty, Lublin, 1968, pp. 504–5.

16. Used at the Inter-University Seminar for the Study of Contemporary Jewry, August 1977, Jerusalem. Franklin H. Littell uses the term "alpine event" in much the same sense—see his *The Crucifixion of the Jews* (New York: Harper & Row, 1975), p. 2. Cf. also Fackenheim's *God's Presence in History* (New York: Harper & Row, 1972).

17. See also, Paul Rassinier, *Le Drame des Juifs Européens* (Paris, 1964).

18. Heinz Roth, *Why Are We Being Lied To* (Witten, 1975); Manfred Roeder, Introduction to Thies Christophersen, *Die Auschwitz-Luege* (Mohrkirch, 1970).

19. United Nations Security Council, S/PV, 1897, March 1976.

20. *New York Times,* 8 October 1977.

21. A. R. Butz, *The Hoax of the Twentieth Century* (Los Angeles: Noontide, 1977).

22. Jiří Bohátka, Třídní Význam Sionismu," two articles in *Tribuna, KSČ týdeník pro politiku a ideologii* (Prague, 1976).

23. See note 20 above.

24. See note 16 above.

25. David Irving, *Hitler's War* (New York: Viking, 1977).

26. Joachim C. Fest, "Revision des Hitlerbildes?" *Frankfurter Allgemeine Zeitung,* 29 July 1977.

27. Lucy S. Dawidowicz, *The War Against the Jews, 1933–1945* (New York: Holt, Rinehart and Winston, 1975).

28. Adolf Hitler, *Hitler's Zweites Buch* (Stuttgart, 1961), pp. 158–59, 220 [in English: *Hitler's Secret Book* (New York, 1962)].

29. Geoffrey Barraclough, *An Introduction to Contemporary History* (Harmondsworth, England: Penguin Books, 1968).

30. Testimony of Yehiel Dinur at the Eichmann trial, in Eduyot, *Mayoetz Hamishpati Lamemshalah neged Adolf Eichmann* (Jerusalem, 1963), pp. 122–23.

31. Cf. Abba Kovner's "Di Shlihes fun di Letzte," a speech delivered on 17 July 1945 at his first meeting with the Palestinian Jewish soldiers in the British army at Tarvisio, Italy. This has been published in a Hebrew translation in Yalkut Moreshet, no. 17 (April 1973), pp. 35–42. An English translation will appear in "The Holocaust—A Generation After," referred to in note 2 above.

CHAPTER 3

1. Emmanuel Ringleblum, *Polish-Jewish Relations during the Second World War* (New York: Fertig, 1976).

2. Władysław Bartoszewski and Zofia Lewin, *Ten Jest z Ojczyzny Mojej* (Krakow, 1966) [in English: *The Blood Shed United Us* (Warsaw, 1970)]; idem, *The Righteous among the Nations* (London: Earlscourt Publications, 1969). Cf. also Kazimierz Iranek-Osmecki, *Kto Ratuje Jedno Zycie . . . Polacy i Żydzi, 1939–1945* (London, 1968).

3. Yisrael Gutman and Shmuel Krakowski's forthcoming study on the subject.

4. Leni Yahil, *The Rescue of Danish Jewry* (Philadelphia: Jewish Publication Society, 1969). For Bulgaria, see note 7 below.

5. David S. Wyman, *Paper Walls: America and the Refugee Crisis, 1938–1941* (Amherst, Mass.: U. of Mass. Press, 1969); Henry L. Feingold, *The Politics of Rescue: The Roosevelt Administration and the Holocuast, 1938–1945* (New Brunswick, N.J.: Rutgers U. Press, 1970); Saul S. Friedman, *No Haven for the Oppressed: United States Policy toward Jewish Refugees, 1938–1945* (Detroit: Wayne State U. Press, 1973).

6. Carl Ludwig, *Die Flüchtlingspolitik der Schweiz* (Bern, 1957). Cf. also Alfred A. Mäsler, *Das Boot ist Voll* (Zürich, 1967).

7. Haim Avni, *Sfarad Vehayehudim* (Kibbutz Meuhad, 1975), and Frederick B. Chary, *The Bulgarian Jews and the Final Solution, 1940–1944* (Pittsburg: U. of Pittsburg Press, 1972).

8. Stronnictwo Narodowe.

9. Statement by the Polish Catholic Press Agency, 25 Jan. 1936; Lukowski in *Sprawe Katolicke*, Lomza, 10 Nov. 1936; Kowalski in *Gazetta Swiateczna*, no. 2915 (1936). I found this material in the JDC Archives, New York, file 46, reports 1936/7.

10. Yehuda Bauer, *My Brother's Keeper: A History of the American Jewish Joint Distribution, 1929–1939* (Philadelphia: Jewish Publication, 1974), p. 235.

11. Yisrael Gutman, *Yehudei Warsha* (Jerusalem, 1977); Ringelblum, *Polish Jewish Relations,* pp. 37–88.

12. Shalom Holavsky, "Hamahteret Hayehudit begettaot Byelorussia Hama'aravit Bi'yemei Ha'shoah" (Ph.D. diss., Institute of Contemporary Jewry, 1977), pp. 27–31.

13. Ibid., pp. 50–52.

14. See Dov Levin, *Lohamim Ve'omdim Al Nafsham* (Jerusalem, 1974), pp. 32-34, for Lithuania, and a forthcoming study by the same author on the Jews in Soviet-occupied territories in 1939–41.

15. Ringelblum, *Polish Jewish Relations,* pp. 182–85.

16. Ibid., p. 218, footnote (footnotes were written by Shmuel Krakowsky).

17. Shmuel Krakowsky, *Halehima Hayehudit Bepolin* (Jerusalem, 1977), p. 29.

18. Ringelblum, *Polish-Jewish Relations,* p. 173; Bartoszewski and Lewin, *Righteous among the Nations,* p. lix.

19. Raul Hilberg, *The Destruction of the European Jews* (Chicago: Quadrangle, 1961), p. 330.

20. Ringelblum, *Polish-Jewish Relations,* p. 312; cf. Hilberg, *Destruction of European Jews,* pp. 297, 301; also, Adolf A. Berman, *Mi'yemei Hamahteret* (Tel-Aviv, 1971).

21. Czesław Madajczyk, *Politika III Rzeszy w Okupowanej Polsce* (Warsaw, 1970), p. 341.

22. Holavsky, "Hamahteret Hayehudit," esp. pp. 306–26.

23. Dr. Helena Kutorgaine, "A Kaunas Diary (1941–1942)," trans. Binyamin Blodz, in *Yalku Moreshet,* no. 17 (February 1974), pp. 31–72; Wila Orbakh, "Hashmadat Hayehudim Beshithei Brit-Hamo'atzot Hakvushim Al-yedei Hagermanim," *Yalkut Moreshet,* no. 19 (June 1975), pp. 109–58; Levin, *Lohamim,* p. 185; for a typical example of a Jewish testimony about Baptists, see *Sefer Yizkor Podhajce (Tel-Aviv,* 1972), pp. 238–39.

24. Livia Rothkirchen, *Hurban Yahadut Slovakia* (Jerusalem, 1961), pp. 14, 24.

25. Cf. Akiva Nir, *Shvilim Bema'agal Ha'esh (Tel Aviv,* 1967), pp. 149–56, for a typical incident of this kind.

26. Frederich B. Chary, *The Bulgarian Jews and the Final Solution, 1940–1944* (Pittsburgh: U. of Pittsburgh Press, 1972).

27. Hilberg, *Destruction of European Jews,* pp. 486–87.

28. Theodor Lavi, *Yahadut Romania Bema'avak Al Hatzalata* (Jerusalem, 1965); also, Lavi, "Hasho'ah" in *Pinkas Hakehillot, Romania,* vol. I, pp. 101–202.

29. Hilberg, *Destruction of European Jews,* pp. 452–58; Dragutin

Rosenberg, "Kurze Karstellung der Jüdischen Verhältnisse in Jugoslawien" (April 1944), in the Saly Mayer Files, JDC Archives, New York. A Ph.D. dissertation now being written at Tel-Aviv University may clarify some of these problems.

30. Massimo Teglio, "Relazione Sull'Attivita Clandestina Della Delasem" (30 October 1945), in Saly Mayer Files, JDC Archives; Lelio Valobra, "Lage der Juden in Norditalien," n.d., in Saly Mayer Files, JDC Archives.

31. Yahil, *Rescue of Danish Jewry.*

32. Betty Garfinkels, *Les Belges Face à la Persecution Raciale, 1940–1944* (Brussels, 1965); Israel Schirman, *La Politique Allemande à l'Egard des Juifs en Belgique, 1940–1944* (Brussels, 1965).

33. Louis De Jong, *Het Koninkrijk Der Nederlanden in De Tweede Wereldoorlog,* vol. 6 (Amsterdam, 1966); Jacob Presser, *The Destruction of the Dutch Jews* (New York: Dutton, 1969); Joseph Michman, "The Controversial Stand of the Joodse Raad," in Yad Vashem Studies no. 10 (Jerusalem, 1974), pp. 9–68.

34. Hilberg, *Destruction of European Jews,* pp. 399–400.

35. Ibid., pp. 389–421; Donald A. Lowrie, *The Hunted Children* (New York: W. W. Norton, 1963); Zosa Szajkowski, *Analytical Franco-Jewish Gazetteer, 1939–1945* (New York: Ktav, 1966); Jacques Ravine, *La Resistance Organisée des Juifs en France* (Paris, 1973). I have summarized much of the material that appeared over the last ten years in *Le Monde Juif,* a journal devoted to the study of the Holocaust and published by the Centre de Documentation Juive Contemporaine in Paris.

36. Based on my research into the material on France in the JDC Archives; cf. also Nili Keren, "Hatzalat Yeladim Betsarfat Bitkufat Hakibush Hagermani" (M.A. diss., Institute of Contemporary Jewry, Hebrew University, 1975), esp. pp. 39–40.

37. Ibid.

38. Rolf Hochhuth, *The Deputy* (New York: Winston, Richard and Winston, 1964); Guenter Lewy, *The Catholic Church in Nazi Germany* (Westminister, Md.: Christian Classics, 1964); Saul Friedlander, *Pius XII and the Third Reich,* trans. Charles Fullman (New York: Knopf, 1966).

39. Michael Dov-Ber Weissmandel, *Min Hametzar* (New York: Emunah Press, 1960), p. 25.

40. English translation in Lucy S. Dawidowicz, *The War Against the Jews, 1933–1945* (New York: Holt, Rinehart & Winston, 1975), p. 149.

41. Yehuda Bauer, *Flight and Rescue: The Organized Escape of the Survivors of Eastern Europe, 1945–48* (New York: Random House, 1970), p. 132.

42. Cf. Dov Otto Kulka, "The Jewish Question in the Third Reich," (Ph.D. diss., Hebrew University, Jerusalem, 1975).

43. Arthur D. Morse, *While Six Million Died: A Chronicle of Americam Apathy* (New York: Random House, 1967).

44. Cf. Charles M. Stember, *Jews in the Mind of America* (New York: Basic Books, 1966).

45. The famous offer by the Dominican Republic's dictator, Trujillo, to accommodate 100,000 Jews in his country was mere eyewash. The JDC tried to establish a settlement at Sosua on the island, and after an expenditure of many millions of dollars, a few hundred European Jews settled there. The settlement was ultimately a failure. See my book *My Brother's Keeper,* pp. 231–36; Feingold, *Politics of Rescue,* pp. 111–13, 122–23.

46. Morse, *While Six Million Died,* p. 8, for the text of the Geneva cable by Dr. Gerhardt Riegner; cf. Yehuda Bauer, "When Did They Know," *Midstream,* April 1968.

47. Ludwig, *Die Flüchtlingspolitik der Schweiz,* pp. 173, 199, 205.

CHAPTER 4

1. Va'adat Ezra Ve'hatzalah; not to be confused with other committees of a similar name in Jerusalem (Va'adat Ha'hatzalah of the Jewish Agency) and in New York (Va'adat Ha'hatzalah of the Orthodox Rabbis in the United States).

2. Grosz had no visa for Turkey, but he was met by representatives of a Hungarian firm that served as cover for espionage activities in Istanbul, "ANTALYA," and they guaranteed him to the Turkish authorities. "A bribe eventually induced the [Turkish] officials to let Grosz and Brand through together, on condition that they went to see Mehmet Bey, President of ANTALYA, in order to settle the question of their entrance visas and residence permits." (Public Record Office, FO 371/42811/WR 422/9/G, interrogation of Andor Grosz, 6–22 June 1944, p. 44 [hereafter cited as PRO/Grosz]).

3. Cf. Raul Hilberg, *The Destruction of the European Jews* (Chicago: Quadrangle, 1961), pp. 542–44, 723–28; Lucy S. Dawidowicz, *The War Against the Jews, 1933–1945* (New York: Holt, Rinehart and Winston, 1975), just mentions the affair in passing, p. 382; Arthur D. Morse, *While Six Million Died: Chronicle of American Apathy* (New York: Random House, 1967), pp. 353–61. The main secondary sources for our story are the following: Joel Brand, *Bishlichut Nidonim Lamavet,* ed. Alex Weissberg (Tel-Aviv, 1957) [hereafter cited as Brand I]; the book also exists in German and English editions: Alex Weissberg, *Die Geschichte von Joel Brand* (Koeln-Berlin, 1956), and Alex Weissberg, *Advocate for the Dead: The Story of Joel Brand* (London: A. Deutsch, 1958); Ernest Landau, ed., *Der Kastner-Bericht* (Munich, 1961) [hereafter cited as Kastner]; Andreas Biss, *Der Stopp der Endloesung* (Stuttgart, 1966) [hereafter cited as Biss]; Henry L. Feingold, "The Roosevelt Adminis-

tration and the Effort to Save the Jews of Hungary" in Randolph L. Braham, *Hungarian Jewish Studies,* vol. 2 (New York: World Federation of Hungarian Jews, 1969), pp. 211–52. Professor Braham's forthcoming study on Hungarian Jewry has not reached me at the time of writing.

4. PRO/FO 371/42811/WR 324/3/48, interrogation of Joel Brand, p. 1 [hereafter cited as Brand II]. This is contested by his cousin, Andreas Biss, who by the way believes his relative to have been a traitor. He claims that Brand never finished his schooling (cf. Biss, p. 40).

5. Ibid., p. 41; Brand I, p. 8, says he returned to Germany in 1930. In his interrogation (Brand II), he says he returned in 1927.

6. Brand II, p. 2.

7. See Randolph L. Braham, "The Kamenets Podolsk and Delvidek Massacres," in *Yad Vashem Studies,* vol. 9 (1973), pp. 133–56.

8. Brand I, p. 14; Brand II, p. 5; Biss, p. 46.

9. Erno Laszlo, "Hungary's Jewry: A Demographic Overview," in Braham, *Hungarian Jewish Studies,* vol. 2, pp. 137–82.

10. Brand I, p. 12.

11. Brand I, p. 54; Bela Vago, "The Intelligence Aspects of the Joel Brand Mission," in *Yad Vashem Studies,* vol. 10 (1974), pp. 111–28; Kastner, p. 42. Other members of the original Va'adah included Zwi (Ernst) Szilagyi of the left-wing Hashomer Hatzair, Eugen Frankel of the Mizrahi, and Moshe Krausz, another Mizrahi member who was in charge of the Palestine Office (the official Jewish Agency office for distributing Palestine immigration certificates). Kastner and Krausz were bitter enemies. A group of Polish refugees, among whom Bronislaw Teichholz was the most prominent, also cooperated with the Va'adah.

12. Kastner, pp. 41, 51–52; PRO/Grosz.

13. Kastner, p. 43.

14. Kastner, p. 56.

15. Heinz Hoehne, *The Order of the Death's Head* (London: Secker and Warburg, 1969), pp. 486–88.

16. Brand I, pp. 56–58; Kastner, pp. 53–57; Brand II, p. 15; JDC Archives, New York, "Claims, Devecseri-Brand," 1955.

17. Kastner, pp. 57–58.

18. Brand II, p. 8.

19. Livia Rothkirchen, *The Destruction of Slovak Jewry* (Jerusalem, 1961), pp. 24–26.

20. Michael Dov Ber Weissmandel, *Min Hametzar* (New York: Emunah Press, 1960), esp. pp. 43–62.

21. Brand I, p. 59, mentions letters by Oskar Neumann, Weissmandel, and Gizi Fleischmann to Baroness Edith Weiss, member of the millionaire Jewish industrialist family, to Freudiger, and to the Va'adah. Kastner, p. 72, mentions two letters, one in Hebrew by Weissmandel, for Baroness Weiss, Freudiger, and Dr. Nissan Kahan,

one of the official leaders of the Hungarian Zionists. Cf. also Shalom Rosenfeld, *Tik Plili 124, Mishpat Gruenwald-Kastner* (Tel-Aviv, 1956), p. 37. Freudiger testified in the so-called "Kastner trial" in Israel (1954) that he met Wisliceny before Kastner and Brand did, that he received Weissmandel's Hebrew letter and read it, and that Wisliceny then asked him to wait until he was summoned. It appears that Wisliceny was trying to find out who the more serious partner for negotiations might be, and that the Abwehr people persuaded him to meet with the Va'adah representatives rather than with Freudiger and his group.

22. According to Kastner, the question posed to Wisliceny through the Abwehr was "is the Jew-commando (*Judenkommando*) prepared to discuss the alleviation of the anti-Jewish steps with the illegal Jewish rescue committee on an economic basis?" (Kastner, p. 71). The story of the contacts appears in Brand I, pp. 61–62; Brand II, p. 16; and Kastner, pp. 71–72.

23. Hilberg, *Destruction of the European Jews,* pp. 528–39; for the missions of Zionist youth leaders, see Joseph Shefer, "Hanhagat Hamahteret Hahalutzit be Hungaria," in *Hanahagat Yehudei Hungaria Bemivhan Hashoah,* ed Y. Gutmann, B. Vago, and L. Rothkirchen (Jerusalem, 1976), pp. 135–49, and also the testimony of Pinhas von Freudiger, March 1975, Oral Documentation Center, Institute of Contemporary Jewry, Hebrew University. The argument put forward by Professor Randolf L. Braham in a paper delivered to a conference in New York in March 1975 ("What Did They Know and When"), takes an opposite line to the one taken here. Braham argues that the Hungarian Jewish leadership, both official and Zionist, should have used their knowledge of what was happening in Poland to warn the Jewish masses and thereby create disorder and panic which might have enabled large numbers of people to escape. It seems to me that this argument is inherently anachronistic in that it fails to recognize the enormous difficulty of changing habits and customs acquired over a long period of time, and the unwillingness of the masses to listen to warnings.

24. Brand II, p. 16. Brand I gives no date, and Kastner gives 5 April. If, however, as Kastner says, Wisliceny was in Bratislava on 24 March, and came back with his letters presumably the next day, then it is doubtful whether he waited over two weeks before acting on them. The earlier date seems to be more likely.

25. Biss, p. 13.

26. See Kastner's testimony in Rosenfeld, *Tik Plili 124* [hereafter cited as T124], pp. 41–42, which elaborates on Kastner, pp. 73–74. Apparently, the idea of a token first shipment of emigrants, which later developed into the so-called "Kastner train" (whose passengers ultimately reached Switzerland via Bergen-Belsen), also was discussed at that

meeting. In the light of the accusation leveled against Kastner by Shmuel Tamir, then defending counsel in the "Kastner trial," that he organized the train in order to save his family and friends, it is interesting to note that in his testimony to the British, Brand claims that the idea was his and he defends it stoutly (Brand II, p. 17).

27. Kastner, p. 73.

28. Compare Kastner, p. 75; Brand I, pp. 65–66; and Brand II, p. 17.

29. Kastner, pp. 77–78.

30. Brand II, p. 18. The difficulty in evaluating the different sources is very real. Brand II is the record of an interrogation, and may not accurately reflect Brand's own words. In addition, he may not have told the British certain details. Three other contemporary statements of Brand are very general and do not specify dates and individuals participating (his meeting with Shertok on 10 June 1944 at Aleppo, his interrogation by Ira Hirschmann (PRO/371/WR 34/3/48), and a brief record of his mission as written down in Istanbul on his arrival (Moreshet Archive, D.1.721). Brand's other two statements are in his book and in his testimony at the "Kastner trial" (actually, the libel suit of Kastner against Malkiel Gruenwald in 1954), both of them ten years after the event. Brand's testimony at the Eichmann trial is of course later still. Kastner wrote his account in 1945, but he was not present at the Eichmann-Brand talks. Eichmann himself presented his side of the story in the Sassen document, published by *Life* in November 1960, and at his trial a year later.

31. Kastner, p. 88, says it was on 8 May. As Kastner was arrested two days later, a date he was likely to remember, it seems reasonable to accept his dating here.

32. Brand II, pp. 23–24.

33. PRO/Grosz, pp. 32–33.

34. Brand II, p. 24.

35. Kastner, p. 88.

36. Brand II, p. 25.

37. Brand II, p. 26, where he says he met Eichmann on Tuesday, 15 May, one day before leaving for Vienna (Wednesday, 17 May). Tuesday was 16 May, of course.

38. Hirschmann (PRO/371/WR 34/3/48), p. 4.

39. Brand I, p. 86; T124, pp. 47–48; Eduyot B., *Hayoetz Hamishpati neged Adolf Eichmann* (Jerusalem, 1963), p. 880.

40. *Life,* 28 Nov. 1960.

41. Brand II, p. 20.

42. PRO/Grosz. Much of the analysis in these and the succeeding paragraphs is based on Bela Vago's brilliant article (see note 11 above). I do not agree, however, with Vago's statement (p. 121) that it was

Grosz who suggested to the SD that Brand be chosen for the mission. Grosz did not know about the mission until Brand was called to Eichmann (see PRO/Grosz, p. 31).

43. Biss, pp. 50–55; Kastner, pp. 88–89. Biss especially shows that Brand helped the SD liquidate the Schmidt group. Both state that Brand was not the right man for the job, and some internal evidence seems to suggest that Brand's wife was of the same opinion. After Eichmann had picked Brand, there was no choice but to agree and give him as much support as possible. Biss describes the consternation of the Va'adah members when they heard that Grosz was to accompany Brand (p. 52).

44. Kastner describes his arrest on 10 May on page 88 of his report.

45. Brand II, p. 30.

46. Moreshet Archives (MA), D.1.714, Menahem Bader to Venia Pomerantz, 27 May 1944.

47. PRO/Grosz, p. 45.

48. T124, pp. 54–65; Brand I, pp. 117–29; Brand II, p. 30; and his talk with Shertok, 10 June 1944, in Ma'ariv, 6 June 1954. Tamir was a politician identified with the Heruth movement. He is presently (1978) Israel's Minister of Justice.

49. T124, p. 56.

50. See note 46 above.

51. MA, D.1.720, Menahem to Venia, 10 June 1944.

52. Brand II, p. 26.

53. PRO/CAB 95/15/JR (44) 11, 30 May 1944, MacMichael's cable of 26 May.

54. *Ma'ariv,* 6 June 1954.

55. MA, D.1.720, 10 June 1944.

56. Ibid.

57. T124, p. 62.

58. See note 54 above. This is confirmed by a cable from Shertok to Goldman in Washington, on 19 June, in War Refuge Board Papers at Hyde Park Roosevelt Library (hereafter cited as WRB), box 70, Pinkerton to WRB, no. 82.

59. WRB, box 70, 7 October 1944, Hirschman conversation with Brand. It seems unlikely that Tamir in 1954, with most of the documentation at his disposal, really believed that Brand was telling the truth. He may have had his own reasons for presenting a distorted picture.

60. See note 53 above.

61. Eduyot, *Hayoetz Hamishpati neged Adolf Eichmann,* pp. 884–86.

62. Brand II, pp. 27–29.

63. See note 54 above.

64. Hirschman, 22 June 1944 (PRO/371/WR/3/48/42807), p. 8.

65. WRB, box 70, Hirschman to Steinhardt, 22 June 1944.

66. U.S., Department of State, *Foreign Relations of the U.S.* (hereafter cited as FRUS) (Washington, D.C.: Government Printing Office, 1944), vol. 1, p. 1050. For what follows, I am indebted to the material and the analysis of David Hadar, "Yahas HaMa'atzamot Lishlihut Yoel Brand," in *Molad,* vol. 4, 1971, n.s., no. 13–14, pp. 112–25.

67. PRO/CAB 95/15/JR (44)13,5/30–31/44. The Cabinet Committee's pompous name was designed to hide the fact that it dealt primarily with Jews. But the initials given to its materials in the Foreign Office spoke for themselves: JR (Jewish Refugees).

68. Hadar, "Yahas HaMa'atzamot Lishlihut Yoel Brand," p. 117.

69. Morse, *While Six Million Died,* p. 313.

70. During the Mayer-Becher negotiations in Switzerland; see my "Onkel Saly—Die Verhandlungen des Saly Mayer zur Rettung der Juden, 1944/45," in *Vierteljahreshefte fuer Zeitgeschichte* (Stuttgart, 1977), Heft 2, April, pp. 188–219.

71. FRUS, 1944, vol. 2, p. 1062.

72. Ibid., p. 1061.

73. Ibid., p. 1074, Harriman's cable of June 19.

74. See note 65 above. Much has been made in popular literature of the remark Moyne is supposed to have made to Brand, regarding the Jews to be saved: "What shall I do with one million Jews? Where shall I put them?" Brand mentioned this in his testimony at the "Kastner trial" (T124, p. 66). In his book (Brand I, pp. 155–56) he tells the story in the text, but then adds a footnote that he found out that the person who he alleges made the remark to him was not Lord Moyne at all. This denial did not prevent Brand from spreading the story later as well. Moreover, the remark itself must be seen in context. The exit of one million Jews from Europe at the time of the Normandy invasion must have seemed to the British utter utopia. At worst, it looked like a desperate ploy of the Nazis to clog up all Allied transport and other resources in the name of a false humanitarianism in order to prevent the Allies from pursuing the war.

75. WRB, box 70, 19 June 1944, Pehle to Morgenthau. The draft of the WRB, dated 13 June is in WRB, box 30.

76. PRO/CAB 95/15//JR (44) 15, 29 June 1944.

77. PRO/371/42807/WR 49/3/48, 28 June 1944.

78. Ibid., 30 June 1944.

79. PRO/371/42807/WR 75/3/48, Berne cable, 26 June 1944; PRO/371/42809/WR 218, Ripka to Nichols, 4 July, and answer by Walker to Ripka, 25 July; PRO/371/42807/WR 48/3/48, cable from Mallet (Stockholm), 2 July; PRO/371/42807/WR 79/3/48, Visser T'Hooft (World Council of Churches in Switzerland) to the Archbishop of Canterbury, 24 June; PRO/371/42811/WR 402/3/48, 19 July, the full report transmitted from Stockholm. Cf. Erich Kulka, "Hamesh Brihot Mi Auschwitz Vehedeihen," in *Yalkut Moreshet* 3 (December 1964), pp. 23–38.

80. WR 48/3/48, in previous note. The Auschwitz report was referred to in Eden's report to the Cabinet on 3 July (42808/WR 169/3/48, Cab Concl. 85 [44]) as a report from Sweden about massacres of Jews. Eden did not doubt the veracity of the report. However, "distressing as the situation was, he doubted if there was any effective action we could take. By issuing warnings to which we could not give effect, we tended to reduce their value."

81. WRB, box 30, Pinkerton to WRB, no. 74, 2 June 1944; WRB box 70, Sternbuch (Harrison) for Union of Orthodox Rabbis, no. 3506, 2 June 1944.

82. PRO/371/42807/WR 49/3/48, Gruenbaum to London, 29 June 1944.

83. Letter of 18 May 1944, in Weissmandel, *Min Hametzar,* p. 93.

84. WRB, box 34, MacClelland to WRB, no. 4041, 24 June 1944. The story of why Auschwitz was not bombed cannot be dealt with in this paper. The British files show that Churchill demanded that everything should be done to prepare for such an action, but the British Air Ministry refused the idea on what it claimed were technical grounds. It was not until 1 September that Weizman got a final negative answer. The Americans replied on 4 July that they could not bomb Auschwitz. In actual fact, Auschwitz was bombed by the U.S. Air Force, on 13 September at the latest, though only the rubber factory (Buna Werke) was attacked. The gas chambers were left unscathed.

85. PRO/371/42808/WR 103/3/48, Aide Memoire of 6 July, and minutes.

86. Ibid., CAB 95/15/JR (44) 19, 12 July 1944.

87. Ibid., JR (44) 17, 4 July 1944, F.O.—Washington, no. 5958, 1 July 1944.

88. PRO/371/42807/WR 75/3/48; and 42809/WR 276/3/48.

89. PRO/CAB 95/15/JR (44) 3rd meeting, 13 July 1944.

90. WRB, box 70, no. 1641, Hull—Harriman, 7 July 1944 (also FRUS, 1944, vol. 2, p. 1089, for the paraphrased version).

91. PRO/CAB 95/15/JR (44) 3rd meeting, 13 July 1944.

92. Ibid., JR (44) 20, 20 July 1944, F.O.—Washington, no. 6460, 18 July 1944(WR 274/10/G).

93. PRO/Grosz. It took the S.I.M.E. (Security Intelligence, Middle East) two weeks to type up a report of no less than a German peace offer. No wonder the British almost lost the war. Bela Vago ("Intelligence Aspects of Joel Brand Mission," p. 125) comments: "Although the S.I.M.E. interrogation reports about Grosz, for instance, were sent to the Foreign Office (or at least extracts of these reports), there is no evidence that they actually reached the highest level and that their contents were duly weighed. . . . one cannot disregard the assumption that the fully-informed British Intelligence Service kept back certain details about the affair, mainly concerning Grosz, from other

competent authorities." This latter statement seems corroborated by additional information now available, but not the first half: the gist of the Grosz mission was transmitted to Eden and formed the basis for the British final rejection of the offer and its subsequent publication.

94. PRO/Grosz, p. 37.

95. Ibid., p. 41. Klages mentioned the name of Nathan Schwalb as the JDC representative. In fact, Schwalb was the representative of Hehalutz, the Pioneering Zionist Youth movement's roof organization. JDC in Switzerland was represented by Saly Mayer.

96. WRB, box 70, no. 274 from Stockholm, 28 July 1944.

97. Cf. Felix Kersten, *Kersten Memoirs* (London: Hutchinson, 1956).

98. T124, pp. 76–89. Grosz tried to commit suicide after the trial. At the time of publication (1978) he is said to be still alive, probably in Germany.

99. MA, D.1.723.

100. WRB, box 70, Emerson on a discussion with Shertok and Linton, 21 July 1944.

101. WRB, box 70, Ben Gurion to Nahum Goldman for Roosevelt, 13 July 1944.

102. MA, D.1.713.

103. PRO/371/42807/WR 102/3/48, and MA, D.1.746 and 721. Cf. also Menahem Bader, *Shlihuyot Atzuvot* (Merhavia, 1954), pp. 110–13; also WRB, box 70, London to Washington, no. 39, 7 July 1944, and no. 5691, 19 July 1944, as well as 13 July, Shertok to Goldman.

104. WRB, box 70, Pehle—Stettinius, 27 July; and Pehle—Norweb, 28 July 1944.

105. Ibid., Pehle memo, 9 July 1944.

106. See note 70 above.

Index